Written by Steve Martin,
Dominique Enright,
Guy Macdonald and Martin Oliver

Illustrated by Martin Remphry,
Simon Ecob and David Shephard

Edited by Bryony Jones, Jen Wainwright,
Hannah Cohen, Samantha Barnes
and Philippa Wingate

Design by Barbara Ward
Cover design by John Bigwood

THE BOOK FOR BOYS

Buster Books

First published in Great Britain in 2013 by Buster Books,
an imprint of Michael O'Mara Books Limited,
9 Lion Yard, Tremadoc Road, London SW4 7NQ

The material in this book was taken from three titles previously published by
Buster Books: *The Boys' Book*, *The Boys' Book 2* and *The Boys' Book 3*

 www.busterbooks.co.uk
Buster Children's Books
@BusterBooks

Text and illustrations copyright © Buster Books 2006, 2008, 2009, 2010, 2011, 2013

Additional illustrations from www.shutterstock.com

A CIP catalogue record for this book is available from the British Library.

ISBN: 978-1-78055-194-4

2 4 6 8 10 9 7 5 3 1

Printed and bound in September 2013 by CPI Group (UK) Ltd, 108 Beddington Lane,
Croydon, CR0 4YY, United Kingdom.

Papers used by Buster Books are natural, recyclable products
made from wood grown in sustainable forests. The manufacturing processes
conform to the environmental regulations of the country of origin.

The publisher and author disclaim, as far as is legally permissible, all
liability for accidents, or injuries or loss that may occur as a result of
information or instructions given in this book

CONTENTS

Note To Readers ... 9

How To Play Air Guitar ... 10

How To Celebrate Scoring A Goal ... 12

How To Talk Like A Pirate ... 14

How To Tie A Bow Tie Like James Bond ... 18

How To Do Some Damage With The Finger Of Doom ... 21

How To Win The Tour De France ... 22

How To Survive A Terrible Haircut ... 26

How To Fall Without Hurting Yourself … Much ... 28

How To Preserve A Tooth ... 30

How to See Through Your Hand ... 31

How To Eat With Chopsticks ... 32

How To Pan For Gold ... 34

How To Avoid Being Eaten By A Polar Bear ... 37

How To Get In And Out Of A Hammock ... 38

How To Eat Spaghetti With Style ... 40

How To Recognize Deadly Snakes ... 42

How To Stop Your Trainers Stinking ... 47

How To Shuffle Cards Like A Pro ... 48

How To Throw A Frisbee ... 50

How To Be A Master Of Disguise ... 52

How To Play A Piece Of Grass ... 55

How To Skid Your Bike ... 56

How To Make A Volcano ... 58

How To Tie A Clove Hitch ... 59

How To Make The Perfect Pizza ... 60

How To Beat A Friend In A Trial Of Strength	63	How To Fake A Spilt Drink	92
How To Escape From An Angry Bull	64	How To Understand What A Dog Is Saying	94
How To Read Body Language	66	How To Toss A Caber	96
How To Open A Coconut	68	How To Make A Cowpat Float	98
How To Whistle Loudly	70	How To Get Rid Of Hiccups	99
How To Avoid Seasickness	71		
How To Make A Shrunken Head	73	How To Ride A Camel	100
		How To Make A Giant Choc-Chip Cookie	104
How To Play The Didgeridoo	76	How To Beat A Gorgon	106
How To Perform A Perfect Round-Off	80	How To Do The Perfect Press-Up	108
How To Talk Like A Pilot	82	How To Fake A Scar	110
How To Be A Ventriloquist	84	How To Play The Toilet Roll	113
How To Pull A Coin From Someone's Ear	86	How To Eat Witchetty Grubs	114
How To Tame A Lion	87	How To Build A Card Tower	116
How To Call Like Tarzan	89	How To Beat A Lie-Detector Test	118
How To Power A Light Bulb With A Lemon	90	How To Speak In Code	119
		How To Save A Penalty	120

How To Make A Balloon Change Colour	122
How To Flip A Pancake	124
How To 'Pop-Up' On A Surfboard	126
How To Catch A Wave	128
How To Ride A Wave	130
How To Shine On Parade	132
How To Receive Your Knighthood	134
How To Go Crabbing	136
How To Survive At Sea	138
How To Navigate By The Stars	142
How To Be A Memory Master	144
How To Be A Kung-Fu King	147
How To Be A Bodyguard	149
How To Make A Magic Cup Of Coffee	150
How To Become A Rock 'N' Roll Drumming Legend	152
How To Be A Superstar Charity Fundraiser	154
How To Be A Frothing-Foam Fighter	156
How To Fly A Kite	158
How To Stop A Nosebleed	160
How To Pitch A Tent	162
How to Read Someone's Mind	165
How To Train Your Goldfish To Play Football	166
How To Make A Coin Go Through A Table	168
How To Make The Perfect Snowball	170
How To Become An Expert	172
How To Draw A Mural	174
How To Survive In Space	176
How To Rip A Phone Directory In Half	179
How To Serve Like A Wimbledon Champion	180
How To Juggle	182
How To Repair A Bicycle Puncture	184
How To Win At Conkers	188

How To Read A Compass   190

How To Shake Off A Tail   192

How To Bend   195
It Like Beckham

How To Keep People   196
In Suspense

How To Jumpshoot   198
A Basketball

How To Recognize   199
A Witch

How To Tell Which Way   200
Is North

How to Warm Your Feet   201

How To Bowl A Spinner   202

How To Customize   204
Your T-Shirt

How To Signal A Plane   206

How To Boil An Egg   210

How To Save The World   213

How To Maximize Your   214
Pocket Money

How To Undo   217
A Jammed Jar Lid

How To Be A Rodeo Star   218

How To Breakdance   221

How To Brew Your Own   224
Ginger Beer

How To Write   227
A Secret Message

How To Ride Bareback   228

How To Be Top Dog   230

How To Annoy People   232
In A Lift

How To Be A Yo-Yo Star   234

How To Win   236
A Nobel Prize

How To Make A Stink   239

How To Make   240
A Mississippi Mud Pie

How To Be   242
A Sound-Effects Wizard

How To Find The Loch   244
Ness Monster

How To Beat The Clock   246
When You Get Up

How To Tell A Good Joke   247

How To Raise Someone   249
Up Using 'Finger Power'

How To Win A Bet   251

How To Putt Like A Pro   254

NOTE TO READERS

The publisher and authors disclaim any liability for accidents or injuries that may occur as a result of the information given in this book.

To be the best at everything, you'll need to use your best common sense at all times, particularly when heat or sharp objects are involved.

Follow safety precautions and advice from responsible adults at all times. Always wear appropriate safety gear, stay within the law and local rules, and be considerate of other people.

How To Play Air Guitar

You've got the looks of a rock god and you've got matching attitude to boot. Unfortunately, you haven't quite saved up enough for a stadium-thumping Fender Stratocaster. Don't worry, air guitar is the one instrument everyone can afford and anyone can play, and here's how.

Mastering The Basics

1. Grab your air guitar. Put the strap around your neck and adjust so it is at the right height for you to play comfortably. Strike some poses in front of a mirror to decide whether you want the guitar to sit high up, level with your hips, or lower down, level with your thighs.

2. Practise strumming. This is the key action for any air guitarist. If you're right-handed, strumming is done by moving your right hand up and down over the 'strings', with your palm facing in towards your body. For a variation, you can pretend that you're holding a 'plectrum' – a small triangle-shaped tool used for plucking the strings individually or strumming.

3. Next practise your chord-playing. Chord-playing is when you play several notes at once. To do this press

down two or more fingers of your left hand firmly against the 'neck' of your air guitar. Move your hand down the neck for high chords and up the neck for lower chords.

4. Select your music. Find a track with long guitar solos so you can really show off your skills. Listen to the track over and over again until you know it by heart. Practise strumming in time to the music, moving your hands up and down the neck to play the high and low bits of the track.

5. Start to move your whole body – head, legs, hips, shoulders – really get into it.

Advanced Air Guitar

As you get more confident, start adopting some more extreme poses. Don't be shy. Remember, the more energetic you are when playing the better. Think about jumps, splits, playing the guitar over your head or behind your back. You could even consider smashing the guitar at the end of your performance.

How To Celebrate Scoring A Goal

How do you make scoring a goal seriously memorable? Easy – just add a special goal celebration afterwards. The secret to creating a spectacular celebration is to be really imaginative and plan it as much as you can in advance.

Don't celebrate an own goal – you won't be popular!

What You Do

Here's a celebration that is easy to carry off.

1. Before the big match, buy or borrow a fabric pen.

2. Dig out an old white T-shirt or vest. Write a short message on the vest. Go for something such as 'Hello Mum' or 'Beckham Junior', or how about 'Pick me next week, Coach'?

3. Once the writing is dry, pack your T-shirt in with the rest of your kit and take it to the game.

4. When no one in the changing room is looking, pop your T-shirt on under your football shirt.

5. Now go out and play your socks off. As soon as you score, start running towards the corner flag or towards anyone in the crowd you particularly want to impress. Untuck your football shirt and pull it over your head so your T-shirt's message can be clearly seen. Spread your arms and keep running until your teammates catch up with you and congratulate you.

Don't crash into the barriers beside the pitch – this is not cool.

We are the greatest!

HOW TO TALK LIKE A PIRATE

There are many reasons you might want to talk like a pirate – maybe you've decided that piracy is the perfect career path for you, you might want to liven up a family boat trip, or perhaps some of your best friends are buccaneers. Whatever the reason, this guide to pirate lingo should give you most of what you need to know to become a true swashbuckling speaker.

Insults

It is important to know these, as pirates spend a lot of time insulting people.

- **Landlubber**
  Anyone who isn't a pirate or sailor.

- **Scurvy Knave**
  Scurvy was an illness pirates got because they didn't have fresh fruit at sea. You don't have to make sure someone has scurvy before using this insult, though – it'll do for anybody.

- **Lily-Livered**
  Cowardly.

Exclamations

Pirate exclamations are useful as you can shout them out at any time you want.

▸ **Shiver Me Timbers!**
Timbers are the wooden beams on a sailing ship. Pirates shout this phrase when they're surprised or annoyed – pretty much any time really.

▸ **There She Blows!**
Usually used when a whale is spotted, but you shouldn't feel limited to whale watching. Use it whenever you like, for example when you see the school bus arriving, when your mum arrives home from work, or when your dinner is ready.

Threats

When pirates are not insulting people, they are usually threatening them. Here are a few useful threats to add to your pirate vocabulary.

▸ **I'll Split Your Gizzard**
I bet you didn't think you had a gizzard, did you? Or that it can be split? Well, a pirate would say that you have, and it can – and it's not very nice.

▸ **Marooning**
A pirate punishment was to leave people on uninhabited islands, known as marooning. Unless your friends have read this book, they may not know what it means, so you can threaten to maroon them even if you don't have a desert island handy.

▸ **Keel-Hauling**
Keel-hauling was horrible. Pirates used to tie someone to a rope, throw them overboard and pull them along underneath the boat. This was very painful indeed as their skin would be ripped off by the barnacles on the bottom of the boat. Threatening to keel-haul someone should be reserved for really, really serious punishments.

Other Useful Words And Phrases

▸ **Me Hearties**
My friends.

▸ **Jolly Roger**
The pirate flag; a black flag with a white skull and crossbones.

▸ **Ahoy!**
Hello!

▸ **Ye**
You. For example, 'I'll split your gizzard, ye scurvy knave, if I don't keel-haul ye first.'

▸ **Be**
Use this instead of 'am', 'is' and 'are'. For example, 'I be a true pirate and ye be a lily-livered landlubber.'

How To Tie A Bow Tie Like James Bond

One of the most amazing things about James Bond – after the stunts, the gadgets and cars – is his ability to look cool when he's wearing a bow tie. If you've ever tried to put one on yourself, you'll know it's easier to wrestle with all sorts of wild animals than tie your own bow tie – until now. Follow the steps on the next two pages to achieve bow-tie perfection.

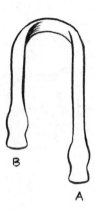

1. Place the tie around your neck, with one end pulled slightly longer (end **A**) than the other (end **B**).

2. Now cross end **A** over end **B**.

3. Take end **A** and tuck it under end **B** and up under your chin, as shown.

4. Take end **B** and make it into a loop.

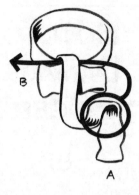

5. Hold the loop with one finger while you bring end **A** over it.

6. Now double end **A** back on itself, pushing it through the loop at the back of the bow tie.

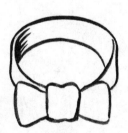

7. For the final 'shaken-but-not-stirred' look, adjust both ends and tighten your perfect bow tie.

MISSION ACCOMPLISHED

How To Do Some Damage With The Finger Of Doom

Gather your friends and tell them that you possess a fearsome finger of destruction – a digit so dangerous you can dent cans with it. All you need is an empty tin can (the kind that beans or tomatoes come in), some friends, a bit of practice and some acting skills.

1. Challenge your friends to dent or crush your tin can in any way, using only one finger (no throwing or stamping allowed). The tin will remain undamaged.

2. Take the tin and lie it on its side on the ground. Inform your audience you will dent it using one finger alone.

3. Put the index finger of your strongest hand across the middle of the tin. Then smack the finger with the palm of your other hand. The tin will dent and you can take a bow.

How To Win The Tour De France

The Tour de France is one of the world's toughest races – it's a worthy challenge for any boy who wants to be the best at everything. Over a period of three weeks, the top cyclists in the world race nearly 3,500 kilometres, sometimes cycling more than 200 kilometres in a single day, riding over some of Europe's most fearsome mountains. If you plan to beat them, there are a few things to bear in mind.

1. Don't cheat! The first winner was Maurice Garin in 1903, who received a hero's welcome when he crossed the finish line. The following year, he won again but was stripped of his title when it was discovered he had sneakily taken the train to arrive first.

2. Eat like a horse. In fact, eat like two horses. A cyclist on the Tour uses about three times more energy than an average man. So, a typical breakfast would be two big bowls of cereal, plenty of fruit, a four-egg omelette and a large bowl of pasta.

3. Don't expect a fantastic prize for winning. The winner receives a jersey. The overall winner gets a yellow jersey, the best young rider gets a white one, and the King of the Mountains (the fastest rider up the mountains) receives a red polka-dot jersey. There is also prize money to be had, but the winner usually gives this away to his team-mates.

Oh great. ANOTHER jersey ...

Top Training Tips

It's important to train properly for the Tour de France, or any cycling event that you're planning on tackling, so that

you can get the most out of it and enjoy it while you're doing it. Follow these top tips to be a cycling superstar:

▸ Make sure your bike's saddle is at the correct height. You should be able to touch the ground with your foot when you tilt the bike slightly.

▸ Take care. A large part of the Tour takes place on roads, but while you're training you should never cycle on your own, and always stay away from busy roads. The best and most fun way to cycle safely is to join your local cycling club.

▸ Don't start by attempting long distances – build up slowly. If you can comfortably cycle three kilometres, try doing five.

▸ When going on a long ride, drink water regularly. Cycling can cause dehydration, which means your body isn't getting enough liquid.

▸ Remember that the Tour de France is a race, and if you want to be in with a chance of winning you need to develop speed as well as endurance. Every now and again while you're cycling, try sprinting as fast as you can for 30 seconds.

▸ Find a nearby hill and practise using your bike's gears. If you use them correctly, you should be able to keep to the same speed as you travel upwards.

▸ What goes up must come down, so it's important to practise a downhill technique, too. When cycling downhill, keep your upper body relaxed and start to brake before any bends to avoid your wheels skidding.

Safe riding is essential. Wear a helmet whenever you are on your bike. It's also a good idea to wear bright clothing, so that you are easily noticed.

HOW TO SURVIVE
A TERRIBLE HAIRCUT

If you've ever been on the receiving end of the haircut from hell, turning you from 'too cool for school' into 'too embarrassed for class', read on for some helpful tips on toughing it out.

Take A Shower
Even the worst hair disasters usually look better after a good soak, shampoo and dry. At the very least, it'll stop your neck itching. At the very best, you might be able to salvage something.

Get Professional Help
Go to your local barber or hairdresser to see if they can repair the damage.

Take Drastic Action
Turn your wonky fringe and tufty clumps of hair into a 'crew cut', a short all-over style. Ask your mum first if you are allowed to have a crew cut. Get a pair of clippers and hand them to someone you trust – a crew cut is almost impossible to mess up. You may have cold ears for a while but at least you'll look cool and save a fortune on gel.

Get A Hat
A terrible haircut is the perfect excuse to get your parents to stump up for that cool baseball cap you've been asking for. Of course, you'll have to take it off at some point but then you can blame your new look on hat-hair!

> If all else fails, don't forget that you will be far more aware of your hair than anyone else. Chances are, no one will even notice that anything's wrong!

How To Fall Without Hurting Yourself ... Much

Are you forever falling over? Well, there's more than one way to tumble, so if you find yourself facing a fall, follow these handy hints to make sure you end up unscathed … well, hopefully.

1. Try to relax and not fight the fall – unless it is clear that falling would lead to serious injury (e.g. if there are unfriendly hazards like rocks or heavy machinery), in which case try to send your body the other way.

2. Try not to land hands down as you could injure your wrists, elbows or shoulders.

3. Attempt to fall on your side rather than your front or back. Half-turn or roll if necessary to land on the fleshier parts of your body.

4. Don't allow your body to open out. Tuck up instead – chin firmly against chest, arms bent at the elbows to protect your head and face.

5. If you're on a bicycle, let go of it, try to swing your leg from under the bike and push the bike away from you.

If you do hurt yourself, make sure you get yourself checked out by a doctor or a health professional.

HOW TO PRESERVE A TOOTH

If you or a friend has a tooth knocked out – playing football, rugby or in an accidental collision – don't panic. These simple steps might help you preserve the tooth long enough for it to be popped back in by a dentist. You'll soon be smiling again.

1. Find your tooth! Don't touch the root. Hold it by the 'enamel' – the hard, white, outer coating.

2. Run home. Clean your tooth thoroughly, rinsing it in milk (not tap water) to remove any blood, earth or grime.

3. Find a clean plastic container with a lid and put the tooth in it. Cover the tooth completely with milk.

4. Take the tooth (and yourself) off to your dentist as quickly as you can (within one to three hours of the accident). If you've followed these instructions, you'll have a 50/50 chance of having your tooth successfully refitted.

How to See Through Your Hand

1. Take a cardboard tube (from a roll of kitchen paper or toilet paper) and look through it with your right eye.

2. Place the edge of your left hand over the end of the tube with its palm facing you.

3. With both eyes open, stare at the point where the tube and the edge of your hand meet and you'll see that you have a hole in your hand.

How To Eat With Chopsticks

Next time you are in a Chinese restaurant, why not leave the knife and fork alone and show off your chopstick skills? The biggest mistake people usually make is to try to pick up their food by moving both chopsticks. If you do this, the food will slip out from between the chopsticks. The trick is to keep one chopstick still and move the other one to meet it. It isn't easy at first, but keep practising and you'll soon be attracting admiring glances from the other diners. Here's how:

1. To hold the first chopstick, place it so it rests at the base of your thumb and the thinner part rests against your ring finger (the finger between your middle and little fingers). This is the chopstick that stays still when you eat.

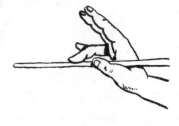

2. Hold the other chopstick between your thumb and index finger in the same way you would hold a pencil. The narrow end should be pointing downwards and there should be about

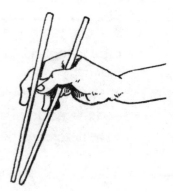

6cm between the tip of your finger and the thin end of the chopstick. You should now be able to press the ends of the sticks together like a pincer, with this second chopstick on top of the other one.

Rice And Easy

If you are eating rice, it would take a long time to pick up the grains of rice between your chopsticks. This is where technique number two comes in.

Hold the chopsticks in the same way as above, but do this so there is a little bit of space between the two ends. Don't move either of the sticks. All you do now is use the two chopsticks to scoop up the rice. The Chinese don't consider it rude if you pick up your plate or bowl and hold it close to your face when you do this.

How To Pan For Gold

Imagine the thrill as, through the mud and the dirt of a stream, you catch sight of something bright, yellow and glittering. Gold!

The following method for finding gold is called 'panning'. Be warned though, the hunt for gold can be extremely addictive, and people have been known to spend their whole lives searching for this moreish metal. If you're

going to try your hand at panning for gold, make sure you don't get taken over by this kind of 'gold fever'.

Don't waste time looking for gold where there isn't any – find a stream where gold has been found before. The most famous 'gold rush', where many people found gold nuggets, was in a river in California in the USA. Do some research online to see if there's a good gold-panning spot near where you live.

You Will Need:
- a metal pan (shaped a bit like a soup bowl)
- a small shovel
- a jar with a lid.

What You Do
1. Find a part of the stream where the water is moving slowly. Panning for gold is about understanding that gold is heavier than the sand, mud and gravel it is found in. The tiny flecks of gold that get swept along by the current sink to the bed of the stream where the water slows down.

2. Using your shovel, dig into the stream bed, lift the dirt out and put it into the pan.

3. Lower your pan into the running water and swirl it around gently. This loosens the sand and stones and the running water carries them away. The gold won't be carried away by the water as its weight makes it sink to the bottom of the pan. You won't get rid of all the sand and pebbles doing this, but you will get rid of most of it.

4. Take the pan out of the water and continue swirling. Tilt the pan slightly so nearly all the water and dirt gradually leave the pan.

5. Use your fingers to search through the remaining material for tiny pieces of gold. If you find any, carefully remove them and put them in your jar.

HOW TO AVOID BEING EATEN BY A POLAR BEAR

▸ To avoid a polar bear in the wild, keep a clean camp. Bears can sniff food and rubbish smells from a long way away. Stay away from mammal carcasses.

▸ Never pet a polar bear cub, no matter how cute it is.

▸ If you are unlucky enough to be approached by a polar bear, stand your ground. Make yourself look bigger by holding a jacket over your head. Shout at the bear.

▸ If all else fails, throw the bear your sandwiches and run.

How To Get In And Out Of A Hammock

Hammocks are brilliant things to have in your garden and make the perfect place to relax and swing gently in the shade.

Unfortunately, getting in and out of a hammock can be the very opposite of relaxing. It's easy to end up flat on your bottom and red in the face. So follow these expert tips to make sure you stay cool at all times.

Getting In

▸ Grip both sides of the hammock and pull the middle area of the cloth taut.

▸ Don't jump on. Instead, lower your bottom on to the area you are holding taut. Rest your weight on your bottom, then lean back slightly, keeping your feet on the ground.

▸ Once your back is on the hammock, slowly swing your legs off the ground and into the hammock.

▸ Try and lie at a slight angle with your head at one side of the hammock and your feet diagonally across it at the other side.

Getting Out

▸ When it's time to get out of your hammock, the first thing to do is turn on to your side.

▸ Slowly move your legs over the edge of the hammock and lower them until they touch the ground.

▸ Hold on to the front edge of the hammock with both hands.

▸ As you transfer your weight from the hammock to your feet, push the hammock away from underneath you.

▸ If you've timed it right, you should find yourself on your feet with the hammock swinging away from you.

HOW TO EAT SPAGHETTI WITH STYLE

Picture the scene … you're staring out of the window of an Italian restaurant. A delicious plate of spaghetti is in front of you and you're starving. You push a small amount of the pasta into your mouth. Mmm, delicious.

But then disaster strikes! You realize that the rest of the sticky spaghetti is hanging down in front of you, smearing tomato sauce all over your chin and your clean, white shirt. At that moment your classmates troop past looking in. Nightmare.

Spaghetti is one of the trickiest foods to eat without making a mess. So you need to be prepared.

Spaghetti Skills

▸ You only need a fork to eat spaghetti – not a fork and spoon, or a fork and fingers – just a plain, simple fork.

▸ Never use a knife to cut the spaghetti up into smaller pieces.

▸ Clear a space near the edge of your dish – you'll need it later.

▸ Take your fork and stick it into the middle of the pasta.

▸ Don't stick it in too far as you don't want to pick up too much. Now, press the prongs of the fork against the plate in the space that you have just cleared.

▸ Twist the fork round and round until the pasta is wound completely round it. There shouldn't be any bits hanging down. If there are, lower your fork, scrape the pasta off against the plate, and try again with a smaller amount of spaghetti.

> If you just can't get a handle on your spaghetti-slurping skills, it might be best to save the dish for when you're eating in private.

HOW TO RECOGNIZE DEADLY SNAKES

If you're travelling somewhere known for its venomous snakes, it's useful to be able to recognize what some experts consider the world's top five deadliest snakes.

> If you get bitten and can identify the snake it will help the paramedics decide which antivenom you need.

The Inland Taipan (Also Known As The Fierce Snake)

▸ **Found In:** Dry, arid regions of Australia.

▸ **Deadly Rating: 1st.** This snake's venom is the deadliest in the world. Just one milligram of its venom is fatal to a human being.

- **Nature:** Generally inactive but will attack if provoked.

- **Appearance:** These snakes can grow up to 1.7 metres long. The back, sides and tail are often pale brown, but the rest of the body is usually black in winter and dark brown in summer.

The Australian Brown Snake
(Also Known As The Common Eastern Brown Snake)

- **Found In:** Australia, Indonesia and Papua New Guinea.

- **Deadly Rating: 2nd.** This snake is responsible for more deaths in Australia than any other.

- **Nature:** Aggressive.

- **Appearance:** They can grow almost two metres long. Mostly brown, they can have patterns on their backs, including multi-coloured bands and speckles. When angry, they hold their necks high in an S-shape.

The Malayan Krait (Also Known As The Blue Krait)

▸ **Found In:** Southeast Asia.

▸ **Deadly Rating: 3rd.** The Malayan krait's venom is 15 times stronger than a cobra's.

▸ **Nature:** Timid in daytime. More aggressive at night.

▸ **Appearance:** This snake can grow up to 1.5 metres in length. Its back has black and white bands that widen as they reach its white underside. The head is greyish, with lighter lips. This snake will often hide its head within its coiled body for protection.

The Tiger Snake

▸ **Found In:** Southern Australia, Tasmania and its coastal islands.

▸ **Deadly Rating: 4th.** If untreated, more than half of bites are fatal.

▸ **Nature:** Aggressive if threatened.

▸ **Appearance:** Tiger snakes grow to about 1.5 metres long. They often have bands, like a tiger, but range in colour from yellow and black to olive- and orange-brown with a paler underside. If threatened, tiger snakes make a loud hissing noise and will raise their heads like a cobra to strike.

The Saw-Scaled Viper

▸ **Found In:** The Middle East, Central Asia, India and surrounding areas.

▸ **Deadly Rating: 5th.** These vipers cause more human deaths than any other snake species.

▸ **Nature:** Aggressive and quick-tempered.

▸ **Appearance:** They grow to about one metre long, and have short pear-shaped heads, with quite large eyes. The scales on their lower sides stick out at an angle of 45°. When threatened, they form C-shaped coils and rub their coils together, making a loud sizzling noise. They move quickly with a side-winding action.

If you do come across any of the snakes listed above, stay calm and try and move slowly out of the snake's range. If you are bitten, get medical help immediately.

How To Stop Your Trainers Stinking

It takes a lot of skill and effort to make sure your trainers have that lived-in 'street' look. The last thing you want is your mum threatening to undo your hard work by washing them, or throwing them in the bin because they're ponging out the house. A few simple steps mean you can have trainers that look good on the outside and smell good on the inside.

▸ **Old Socks.** Fill a pair of old, clean socks with some cat litter (clean cat litter, of course). Stick a sock in each trainer and leave them overnight.

▸ **Tea Leaves.** Try putting loose tea into each trainer. Shake it all out in the morning.

▸ **Bicarbonate Of Soda.** Put a teaspoon of this in each trainer and shake it around. Leave overnight then shake out into the bin.

▸ **Orange Peel.** Pop some into your shoes overnight, and remove it the next morning.

How To Shuffle Cards Like A Pro

Shuffling cards using the 'Riffle Shuffle' is a great chance to impress your friends with your coolness. This looks difficult – which is why it will impress everyone – but only takes a little bit of practice to get right.

What You Do

1. Split the pack in half. The cards only need to be split roughly in half, so there's no need to count them out.

2. Take one half in your left hand, holding the top of the half-deck with your thumb and the bottom with your middle finger. Do the same to the other half of the deck with your right hand.

3. Hold the two half-decks upside down and next to each other, just above a table.

4. Push the decks into a curve by pressing the knuckle of your index finger into the back of them. Lean the cards on the table if necessary.

5. The next part takes a little practice to get right. Fire the cards down on to the table, releasing them smoothly by curving your thumb slowly away. The cards should spring down so that, as cards from your left hand land on the table, cards from your right hand interweave with them. This continues until all the cards are on the table and mixed up.

6. Carefully lift up the two half-decks, one in each hand. You could just slide them together into one deck now, but not if you want to look like a real card-shuffling pro. So, push the cards in slightly and then, resting your thumbs on the top of the decks, place your other fingers underneath and bend the decks upwards.

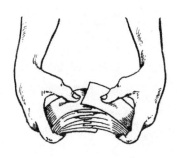

7. Finally, let go with your fingers and push down with your thumbs while pressing your palms inwards. The cards will spring together into one pack.

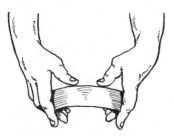

How To Throw A Frisbee

Some skills mark out the cool people from everyone else, and one of these is being able to throw a Frisbee. There are three things to get right if you are going to do this well – gripping the Frisbee, swinging your arm, and throwing the Frisbee.

Note. The instructions below are for right-handed people. If you are left-handed, simply reverse the left and right instructions.

The Grip

Hold the Frisbee with your palm against the rim, your fingers wrapped round the rim and your thumb on top. Your wrist should be curled slightly inwards, towards your body.

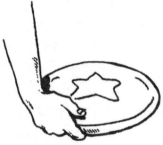

The Swing

Your arm should be across your body. Hold the Frisbee in your right hand and bring your right arm across your chest so the Frisbee is to the left of your body.

The Throw

Move your arm away from your body and release the Frisbee when the angle between your arm and your body is about 45°. Release it with a quick snap of the wrist. It is your wrist that provides the power to make the Frisbee fly.

Top Throwing Tips

▸ Look at the person you are throwing to, not at the Frisbee.

▸ The Frisbee must be level when you release it. It should not tilt down, or to the left or right.

▸ Your movements should be nice and smooth. There is no need to throw it as hard as you can. The chances are this will just make the Frisbee fly off in the wrong direction.

HOW TO BE A MASTER OF DISGUISE

Disguising yourself is a useful skill if you want to throw someone off your tracks or follow someone you know without being recognized.

A good disguise will simply allow you to move around unnoticed. To do this, it's a good idea not to draw attention to yourself. The less noticeable you are, the less time people will spend looking at you and the more successful your disguise is likely to be.

Be Prepared

Think carefully about what you need to create your disguise and whether it will all fit in your rucksack or school bag. You never know when you might need it. Here are a few ideas for your portable disguise kit:

- reversible jacket or top
- hat
- glasses or sunglasses
- comb
- styling gel

- baggy clothes
- cotton-wool balls
- stick-on tattoos
- fake nose
- a wig.

Make sure your wig is a different style or colour to your real hair – your local fancy-dress shop should be able to supply you with one.

Change Your Body Shape

If you're a bit on the skinny side, try to make yourself seem fatter. Wear extra layers of clothing – this will also

change the way you move. Puff out your cheeks or put a grape into each cheek to change your face shape.

If you're not very tall, try to make yourself seem taller. Wear shoes with heels rather than flat shoes, spike up your hair and don't slouch. Alternatively, you could always try hunching your shoulders to change how you look from behind.

Change Your Walk

If possible, ask a friend to video you walking. This is a great way to see what other people see. Analyse your movements and think hard about how you could change them.

If you usually bounce along full of energy, try to slow yourself down. Walk more slowly and make your movements heavy and more clumsy.

If you walk slowly already, practise walking faster. Try walking on the balls of your feet or leaning forwards. Ask your friend to video your new walk and see if you can see the difference. You could try taking bigger steps when you walk, or even adopting a slight limp.

Change Your Talk

The way you talk and interact with other people is often a real give away. Try to change small things about your voice, by speaking more slowly or at a lower pitch. Talking in a higher pitch might just make you laugh!

Confidence Is Key

The most important thing, however you disguise yourself, is to act natural and confident. Nothing will give you away faster than if you are hesitant or awkward in your new disguise – this will quickly arouse suspicion.

HOW TO PLAY A PIECE OF GRASS

Don't play an instrument? Well how about learning to play a blade of grass?

1. Find the tallest and widest piece of grass you can.

2. Press the sides of your thumbs together, with the nails facing towards you.

3. Place the piece of grass between your thumbs, so that it runs from top to bottom.

4. You will now be able to see a strip of grass in the gap between your knuckles and where your thumbs meet your hands.

5. Blow through the gap. If you don't hear a whistle at first, adjust your lips and the grass, and keep trying.

How To Skid Your Bike

S kidding the back wheel of your bike, also known as a 'Side Skid', is a simple but effective stunt you can do with just a little practice. It makes for a pretty impressive entrance.

Before You Start

▶ Your bike should be in good condition, with the tyres pumped up and with good treads on them.

▶ Your brakes should be working well, and you must wear safety gear, such as elbow and knee pads and a helmet.

▶ You need a hard surface for skidding, so choose an unused stretch of tarmac or a concrete area in a playground. Make sure there are no other vehicles using the area before you attempt a skid.

Performing A Side Skid

1. Start by pedalling fairly slowly, travelling roughly the same speed as a slow jog. Once you've mastered the technique, you can go faster.

2. Move your weight forwards off the back wheel and lean slightly to the right as if you're about to go round a corner.

3. Take your right foot off the pedal, and hold it straight out to the side, just above the ground. Then brake hard with your back brake (the back brake is usually operated by the brake on the left-hand side of your handlebars, but it can vary).

4. You should feel the back tyre trying to grip the ground, and the bike will begin to rotate, skidding to the left. As your bike comes to a standstill, put your right foot down to steady yourself.

5. Practise the side skid, building up your speed gradually, for a more impressive and longer-lasting skid.

How To Make A Volcano

Here's some spectacular science for you to make an explosive mess with at home.

You Will Need:
- modelling clay (brown and red are best)
- baking soda
- red food colouring
- washing-up liquid
- vinegar.

1. Make a volcano shape with the modelling clay. Use brown clay for the base and red clay for the rim to look like hot lava. If you can't find red clay, colour a small amount with the food colouring.

2. Scoop out a hole in the top of the volcano for the crater. Put one tablespoon of baking soda, a few drops of red food colouring and a few drops of washing-up liquid in the crater.

3. Pour in ¼ cup of vinegar, stand well back and watch the volcano erupt.

This is a messy project and needs space, so if you can, make it outdoors or cover your work area with newspaper.

How To Tie A Clove Hitch

A 'clove hitch' is one of the most useful knots you can learn, allowing you to attach a rope to almost anything. Use a clove hitch to moor a boat, secure a rope when rock climbing, or simply attach a piece of string to a paper clip!

Practise the simple steps below to attach a piece of rope to a rock-climbing clip, known as a 'karabiner'.

1. Make two identical loops with your rope.

2. Slide the loop on the right in front of the loop on the left.

3. Open the karabiner's gate (the clip part) and lift the two loops through the gate. Pull both ends of your rope down to tighten the clove hitch.

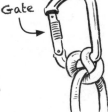

Gate

How To Make The Perfect Pizza

Are you bored of the same old, tired pizzas that you can buy in the shops? Here's a solution.

Fresh, home-made pizza is truly delicious, and if you think it's difficult to make, think again. Home-made pizza is easy, fun and very tasty. Follow these simple steps and you'll be cooking like a real Italian pizza chef in no time.

Before you start, remember the golden rules of cooking: always get permission from your parents and get an adult's help when dealing with hot ovens and sharp knives.

You Will Need:
- 200g plain flour
- 1 teaspoon dried yeast
- a pinch of salt
- a pinch of sugar
- 1 tablespoon olive oil
- 120ml warm water
- olive oil for brushing round the bowl
- 2 tablespoons tomato purée
- 150g grated cheese
- some extra tasty toppings (see page 62).

What You Do

1. Pour the flour into a bowl and mix with the yeast. Add the salt and sugar.

2. Make a little dent in the middle and pour in the olive oil and water. Mix together with your hands until you have a lump of dough.

3. Take the dough out of the bowl and put it on a hard surface that you have sprinkled with flour (this will stop the dough sticking).

Grab the edge of the dough and fold it over the rest of the dough. Push down into it with the heel of your hand to flatten it. Turn it round a little bit and do this again. This is called 'kneading' the dough, and you should knead for a few minutes.

4. Rub some olive oil around the bowl to stop the dough sticking. Put the dough back in and cover the bowl with a cloth. Leave it for an hour, so the dough has time to rise (this is what happens to dough when you put yeast in it).

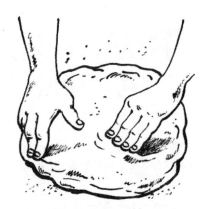

5. Take the dough out and knead it again to get rid of any large air bubbles. Then press and shape the dough with your fingers into a circular pizza shape.

6. Spread the tomato purée over your base and sprinkle the grated cheese over the top of it.

Get 'Topping-Tastic'

Now, the fun really starts – adding the toppings. You can add toppings you are familiar with, such as ham and pineapple, or you can invent completely new pizza flavours. What about a beef and barbecue sauce pizza, or a smoked salmon and cream cheese pizza?

Once the toppings are on, place your pizza on a baking tray in the oven at 220°C (Gas Mark 7) for about 15 minutes. When you take it out, the crust should have browned and the cheese should be bubbling.

How To Beat A Friend In A Trial Of Strength

If any of your friends think they are really strong, you can prove your superior strength with this simple test.

Egg-Stra Strong

1. Ask your friend if he thinks he can break an egg with his bare hands. Of course, he will say, 'Yes'.

2. Ask him to take the egg in one hand, wrap his fingers evenly around it and squeeze it as hard as he can. To his amazement, he will find that the egg is indestructible. This is because, although eggs can be easily broken by hitting them, they are actually designed to take quite a bit of squeezing. If this wasn't the case, they would break when they were being laid.

3. Now it's your turn. The trick is to make sure that you are wearing a ring. One squeeze and the egg will break. When you press the eggshell, all the pressure is on one point – the ring. When your friend tried, the pressure was evenly spread out all around the egg.

HOW TO ESCAPE FROM AN ANGRY BULL

Next time you're out in the countryside, keep your eyes peeled and stay out of fields that contain any large, menacing bull-like shapes. However, if you do find yourself facing an angry bull, here's what to do.

Stay Still

Don't approach it, and do everything you can to stop the bull noticing you. Resist any instinct to run. A bull can smell and hear better than people, but it can't see very well. If you move, that will attract its attention.

Always keep the bull in sight. Once it has moved away or doesn't seem interested in you any more, start heading slowly and steadily towards the gate.

Charge!

If the bull is heading your way, it's time to run. Bulls can easily outrun a person. As a result, you need to look for cover in a nearby building or behind a solid gate or fence.

As the bull charges towards you, try to distract him. Take off your jacket and swing it in the air to attract the bull's attention. Then, before the bull gets too close, throw your jacket as far away from yourself as possible. The bull should go to investigate it rather than you. Repeat with as many layers of clothing as you have until you reach safety.

Don't panic if you are wearing red – bulls don't react to red any more than any other colour.

How To Read Body Language

Think about how many things you say in an average day. It may amaze you to know that you communicate even more through body language than through speech.

Understanding body language helps us discover what people really mean and how they really feel. Someone might say one thing, but body language signals may tell a different story. We all know a smile means happiness or friendliness, and crying means sadness, but here are some less well-known signals to look out for.

Decisions, Decisions

▸ If a person is stroking his chin, he is thinking about something and trying to make a decision.

▸ If he is tugging his ear, it means he can't make his mind up.

▸ If you try to help by making a suggestion and he pinches his nose and closes his eyes, it means he doesn't think it is a good idea.

Liar! Liar!

Tell-tale signs of lying can be difficult to spot, but clues someone may be lying to you include the person:

▸ Looking away to the left

▸ Covering his mouth with his hand while speaking

▸ Rubbing his nose

▸ Turning away from you.

I'm The Boss

Some people show who's in control of a situation through their body language. Here are the signs to look for:

▸ If someone leans back and puts his hands behind his head, he thinks he is in control.

▸ He might also use his hands to make a steeple shape to show he's in charge.

▸ Someone standing with his hands on his hips means he feels ready to take on anything. Be careful, though, as it can also be a sign of aggression.

World-Wide Body Language

Another important point to remember is that body language can change depending upon which country of the world you are in. In Chile, showing someone your hand with your palm facing upwards and your fingers spread out means you think that they are stupid, and in Thailand, showing the soles of your feet is seen to be very rude indeed. So, as well as learning to read the body language of those around you, you should always check your own body language to make sure you're not sending out the wrong signals.

HOW TO OPEN A COCONUT

There's nothing that sums up the taste of the tropics as much as cool coconut milk and the wonderful flavour of white coconut. If you should find yourself feeling peckish while on a tropical island paradise, then you need to crack the method for opening a coconut to get at the delicious food inside.

Here's How:

1. First, pull off the hairy layer around the outside of the coconut with your fingers.

2. Look closely at the coconut. You will see three black spots, each the size of a small coin. These are the coconut's weak spots. Push a sharp stick through two of these holes and hold the coconut over a container to let the milk drain out.

3. There is a line, called a 'seam', running between the top two black spots. Follow this to the middle of the coconut, then form an imaginary line around the fattest part of the middle.

4. Tap the coconut sharply with a rock all the way around this imaginary line. The coconut should soon break apart into two halves.

5. Once your coconut is open, you can carefully cut the white bits away from the shell. Check that they don't smell sour or mouldy, and then pop them into your mouth.

How To Whistle Loudly

Whistling in tune is all well and good, but sometimes you can't beat a really loud whistle to grab someone's attention or show your appreciation. Here's how you do it.

1. 'Wet your whistle' or take a drink of water. Learning to whistle loudly can be a thirsty business.

2. Use the thumb and index finger of one hand to make a 'U' shape. Leave about a half-centimetre gap between the tips. Put your fingers in your mouth.

3. Curl your lips back against your teeth and around your fingers. Leave only a tiny bit of your lips visible. Make sure they are stretched tight.

4. Press your tongue down just behind your bottom teeth. You should have a small bump in the middle of your tongue while the front of it should be wide and flat.

5. Breathe in through your nose then blow air out through the small gap in your fingers. Use the top of your tongue to guide the air. You may find that pushing down with your fingers on your bottom lip and teeth helps. Keep practising until you can position everything perfectly and adjust your breath for maximum whistling volume.

How To Avoid Seasickness

Up and down! Side to side! You thought your Caribbean cruise would be the holiday of a lifetime, but instead you're feeling rotten. You've been hit by the traveller's curse: seasickness. When you board a ship, you are moving into a world where nothing stays still, which confuses your brain and body and can make you feel ill.

Until you've been on a sea voyage, you won't know whether you suffer from seasickness or not. However, there are things you can do to help avoid seasickness or to get over it quickly if you become unwell.

▸ Until you have been at sea for a few hours, you should avoid going below deck. Spend as much time as possible gazing out at the horizon, where the water meets the sky. The horizon is a fixed point, so looking out at it helps your brain get used to being at sea.

▸ If you do feel unwell, it can help to lie down, but do not lie down in your cabin. Find a comfortable deckchair and lie on deck. Make sure somebody stays with you.

▸ If you are on a cruise, you will be tempted by all sorts of wonderful, exotic food. Try not to give into temptation during your first day. Eat lightly and eat familiar food.

▸ If you do get seasick, you will get better. Once at sea, your brain and body will get used to the movement of the ship.

Many experienced travellers say ginger is a good remedy for seasickness. Why not take some ginger biscuits with you when you board?

How To Make A Shrunken Head

There was a time when certain tribes would attack their enemies, cut off their heads, take the severed heads home as trophies and shrink them. The problem with doing this is that it is dangerous, cruel, very messy and could get you into a lot of trouble. Because of this, here's a shrunken-head method that uses an apple. The result looks just as good and you don't have to go to all the bother of chopping someone's head off.

You Will Need:
- a large apple
- 600ml water
- 60g salt
- 30cm string
- coloured chalk
- potato peeler
- a small knife
- 2 tablespoons lemon juice
- wooden or metal skewer.

What To Do:

1. Carefully remove the peel of the apple using a potato peeler.

2. Use a small knife to create the face. Ask an adult to help you. Remember that the head is going to be shrunk, so make the features a bit bigger than you normally would.

Make each eye quite deep set as this helps to give the shape of the nose, sticking out from the face.

Shape the mouth so the two lips stand out. A nice deep cut between the lips will help them to separate during shrinking.

3. Take a bowl and add the water, salt and lemon juice. Stir until the salt has dissolved, then put the apple in. The head needs to be completely covered by the liquid. If it isn't, add more of the above mixture.

4. To make sure the apple stays completely covered by the liquid at all times, place a plate on top of the bowl.

5. You now need to show a little bit of patience as you have to leave your 'head' in the liquid for a full 24 hours ... the apple head, that is – not your own head!

6. The next bit needs a lot of patience, as the head will take about three weeks to dry. Stick the skewer through the top of the apple, and tie a piece of string to the top of the skewer.

Hang it up somewhere it won't be in the way. It needs to be hung up so that the air can get to every side of the apple and stop it from going mouldy.

7. Finally, your shrunken head is ready to decorate. Use coloured chalk to colour in the head and features.

To make your head even more realistic and gruesome, use glue to add some raisins for the eyes and pieces of rice for teeth.

HOW TO PLAY THE DIDGERIDOO

The cool kids at school play the guitar, your mum wants you to play the piano, your teacher suggests something else again. Why not ignore them all and learn to play … the didgeridoo?

The didgeridoo is the instrument famously played by the Australian Aborigines (the earliest inhabitants of Australia), and is one of the world's oldest instruments. It might sound unbelievable, but the didgeridoo is actually made by insects.

The instrument is made from a branch from the Eucalyptus tree. Australian termites hollow out the branches of the tree and the Aborigines cut the branch when the thickness of the wood is just right for a didgeridoo.

While you might not have a real didgeridoo to play, you can still practise the technique. Try using the long cardboard tube from a roll of wrapping paper as your makeshift didgeridoo.

The most important part of playing the didgeridoo is mastering the drone. This isn't the same kind of drone that teachers are so good at; it's the name given to the loud, continuous humming sound produced by the didgeridoo.

What You Didgeri-Do

1. Kneel down with your didgeridoo in front of you. Hold it in one hand with the mouthpiece close to your mouth and the other end resting on the floor. Keep your back straight, so that the didgeridoo is at an angle of roughly 45°.

2. Before you try and get any noise out of the instrument, it's important that your lips are properly relaxed. If you try blowing into the didgeridoo with lips that are too tight, you'll end up producing a seriously uncool squeaking sound.

Practise blowing with relaxed lips. You will look like you are doing an impression of a horse, and the noise you make should sound like you're blowing a raspberry.

3. Once you've got your lips loose and relaxed, it's time to start making some noise. Position your lips on the didgeridoo so you have a tight seal around the mouthpiece. Blow straight into the mouthpiece, keeping your lips relaxed at all times.

If you get this right, you'll hit what is known as the 'sweet spot', and will produce a deep, resonant drone. This drone will be the basis for your music, and you will need to keep it going in one long, continuous sound.

Circular Breathing
Now, unless you've got serious lung power, you will certainly run out of breath. So, you need to learn the didgeridoo player's technique of circular breathing.

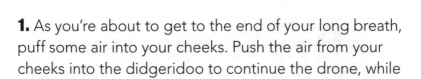 

1. As you're about to get to the end of your long breath, puff some air into your cheeks. Push the air from your cheeks into the didgeridoo to continue the drone, while taking a deep breath in through your nose.

2. Now you will be able to start another long exhale into the didgeridoo without having to cause a break in the sound that you're making. Circular breathing can be quite tricky, so don't worry if it takes you lots of practice.

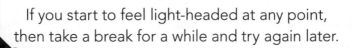

If you start to feel light-headed at any point, then take a break for a while and try again later.

Music Maestro

1. Now you should be droning nicely, and you are ready to add some variety to the noise you're making. Form the letter 'D' repeatedly, tapping your tongue against the roof of your mouth while continuing your drone. This is known as the 'kangaroo hop' and will add some rhythm to your music.

2. If you want to change the pitch of your drone, try loosening and tightening your lips as you blow, while keeping your tongue against the roof of your mouth. This will create a range of different sounds.

How To Perform A Perfect Round-Off

A 'round-off' is a more impressive stunt than a cartwheel, but it takes a bit longer to master. It starts off exactly the same as a cartwheel, but you should bring your feet together while you are upside down and land facing the direction you came from.

Follow the steps below to perfect your round-off. Make sure you practise on a gym mat.

1. Start with your right foot forwards if you are right-handed (left foot forwards if you are left-handed). Extend your arms above your head as shown.

2. Lunge forward, placing both hands on the mat, one after the other (as if you were going to do a cartwheel). Kick your legs up, one-by-one, until they end up side-by-side stretched vertically above your head for a moment.

3. Twist your body as you snap your legs back down to the mat.

4. When you land on the mat you should be facing the direction from which you came.

Bend your knees slightly as your feet hit the mat. If you find yourself off balance when you land, add a small jump. This will look like part of the move.

How To Talk
Like A Pilot

If you've ever listened in on a pilot's conversation, you'll know they use a special system to spell out words. It's known as the 'spoken phonetic alphabet' and is used to avoid confusion during intercom conversations. Learn the alphabet below off by heart so you can use it in emergency situations or when it is vital you are understood.

A	Alpha	**J**	Juliet	**S**	Sierra
B	Bravo	**K**	Kilo	**T**	Tango
C	Charlie	**L**	Lima	**U**	Uniform
D	Delta	**M**	Mike	**V**	Victor
E	Echo	**N**	November	**W**	Whisky
F	Foxtrot	**O**	Oscar	**X**	X-ray
G	Golf	**P**	Papa	**Y**	Yankee
H	Hotel	**Q**	Quebec	**Z**	Zulu
I	India	**R**	Romeo		

Here are a few useful words that might come in handy:

Mayday: 'Help!'

Roger, Out: Ends a conversation.

Ten-Four: Confirms you have understood the message.

Sit-rep: Stands for 'situation report', such as 'where are you?', 'is anybody injured?' etc.

How To Be A Ventriloquist

Ventriloquists use their voices and their powers of illusion to bring a dummy to 'life'. To become a good ventriloquist you will need to convince an audience that the dummy is talking, not you. Here are some basic skills you need to master.

Don't Move Your Lips

It's almost impossible to speak without moving your lips at all, so don't worry if you struggle with this. However, it is important to restrict your lip movements as much as possible.

Sit in front of a mirror and hold a finger to your lips as if making a 'shushing' gesture. Say the sounds of the alphabet out loud. You will notice that some letters make your lips move more than others. The worst offenders are usually 'b', 'p', 'm' and 'w'.

What you have to do is substitute these letters with similar sounds that won't make your lips move so much. Now, try saying 'd' for 'b', 'kl' for 'p', 'n' for 'm' and 'ooh' for 'w'.

This will sound odd at first, but keep practising and you'll find that you are able to slip these substitutes into words without other people noticing.

Don't Be A Dummy!

A ventriloquist's dummy is vital to the success of an act. It distracts the audience's attention from your mouth by looking and sounding funny.

You can use anything from an old doll to a well-loved teddy bear as your dummy. However, a sock puppet (a sock with two eyes sewn on it and a 'mouth' operated by your thumb in the toe of the sock) is great to practise with, as you can get used to moving the dummy's mouth in time with the words you are speaking.

Change Your Voice

Don't forget that the trick to ventriloquism is to fool your audience into thinking that your dummy is talking, not you. One of the ways to do this is to give your dummy a voice that is different to your own, so practise changing the tone and the speed at which you usually talk. Always practise in front of a mirror so you can check how visible your lip movements are.

How To Pull A Coin From Someone's Ear

This is a trick that every magician should know. With some simple hand movements you'll be able to convince your friend that you have produced a coin from his ear. Here's how to do it.

1. Take a coin in your right hand and show it to your friend. Make sure you also show them that your other hand is empty.

2. Turn your right hand over, and pretend to transfer the coin from your right hand into your left one. Close your left fist around the imaginary coin, and move your right hand (which still has the coin in it) down by your side.

3. Ask your friend to blow on your left hand, then open it to show that the coin has magically vanished.

4. Bring your right arm up and place your hand behind your friend's ear.

5. In one fluid motion, slide the coin from the palm of your right hand into your fingertips, and bring the coin out from behind your friend's ear. Magic!

HOW TO TAME A LION

Cats are usually affectionate animals that make great pets, but if you're planning on becoming a lion tamer you have to be a bit careful. The pussy cat you'll be dealing with is over a metre tall, weighs 200kg and has teeth that could tear your head off! The three vital skills a lion tamer needs are caution, bravery and patience. Here's how to teach your lion to do a trick.

Jumping Through Hoops
▸ It is very important that the lion trusts you. Lion tamers often raise their lions from cubs, which gives them a strong bond.

▸ You are going to teach the lion to respond to a signal. Put a hoop in front of the lion with a toy or bright object on the other side of it. Step back and click your fingers.

▸ At this point, the lion doesn't know what you are trying to do. If it does step through the hoop to investigate the object on the other side, reward it immediately with some food. If not, be patient until it does. Don't make the lion angry by trying to hurry it.

▸ Keep doing this exercise, and every time the lion steps through the hoop, give a food reward.

▸ You will soon find that the lion will step through the hoop when you click your fingers even when the toy is not there. Well done, you have successfully tamed your lion.

How To Call Like Tarzan

Everyone knows that Tarzan is King of the Jungle, famous for wrestling crocodiles and swinging from trees. But he is most famous for his amazing jungle call. Here's how you can recreate it.

▸ Find somewhere you can practise without disturbing your friends and neighbours (it might be best to make sure you're not close to a zoo, just in case). Fill your lungs with air, then make an 'ahhhh' sound from the back of your throat.

▸ After a couple of seconds, gently beat the top of your chest with your fists. This will cause your voice to change, creating a yodelling effect. Beating different areas of your chest will make different sounds.

▸ Try to maintain the call for at least ten seconds, and vary it by changing the flow of your breath.

How To Power A Light Bulb With A Lemon

Everyone talks about green power, but here's a little 'yellow' power. Read on to discover how you can turn on a light bulb with a lemon.

You Will Need:

- a large, fresh lemon
- a pair of pliers
- a zinc screw about 5cm long
- a copper screw about 5cm long
- a set of old Christmas-tree lights.

What You Do

1. First of all, you need to get the juice flowing inside the lemon by gently squeezing or rolling it on a hard surface. Don't break the skin – you don't want any juice to escape.

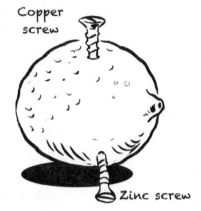

2. Screw the zinc screw into one side of the lemon and the copper screw into the opposite side. Don't screw them all the way through, and don't allow them to touch each other in the middle. You are aiming to leave them so that the ends of the nails are about two centimetres apart inside the lemon.

Copper screw

Zinc screw

3. Use the pliers to snip one of the Christmas tree light bulbs off from the set. Make sure you leave about five centimetres of wire on either side of the base of the bulb. Ask an adult for help with this.

4. Now carefully peel away about 2.5 centimetres of the plastic insulation from the light's wires to expose the metal wires beneath.

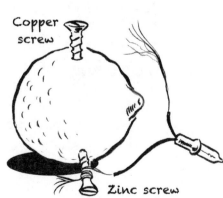

Copper screw

5. Once the end of each wire is exposed, wrap one bare end around the zinc screw.

Zinc screw

6. Dim the lights in the room and close the curtains or blinds. Quickly wrap the bare end of the other wire around the copper screw.

7. Look carefully and you'll see that the bulb has been illuminated by the lemon-yellow power. The acid in the lemon juice creates a chemical reaction when it touches the metal, producing energy. This energy is enough to light the bulb.

How To Fake
A Spilt Drink

H ere is an excellent practical joke that will temporarily cause panic at the dinner table.

You Will Need:
- a paper cup
- PVA glue
- orange food colouring
- an old plastic bag
- scissors.

What You Do
1. Take a cup and pour in about a tablespoon of PVA glue. Add a few drops of orange food colouring to create the look of spilled orange juice. Stir.

2. Spread the plastic bag out on a flat surface. Tip the cup on one side and dribble glue out of the cup to make the shape of a liquid spill on the plastic bag. Make sure the cup is resting on the plastic bag and touching the edge of the 'spill'. Leave the glue to set.

3. Once the glue is dry, cut around your spill with scissors.

Wait until the table is laid for a special occasion, then position your spill. You might need earplugs for when your trick is discovered.

How To Understand What A Dog Is Saying

Although dogs can't actually speak, this doesn't mean you can't understand what they are telling you. Dogs are descended from wolves and are used to being in a close group, called a pack. They need to be able to communicate with other pack members so they can explain what they want, and work out who's in charge.

Most dogs live with humans nowadays and will communicate with them just as if they were other dogs. The main method they use to 'speak' is body language.

Opposite is a useful Dog to Human dictionary to help you make sense of your canine friends.

MOVEMENT	MEANING
Putting part of his body on top of yours – for example a paw resting on your leg	I'm the boss
Patting you with his paw	You're the boss
Lying down watching you	You're the boss
Rolling over so you can rub his stomach	You're the boss
Tearing up things while you're out	I'm upset because you left me on my own
Putting his front feet on the floor with his front legs stretched out and his bottom in the air	I want to play
Bright, alert eyes and relaxed lips, or his tongue hanging out	I'm happy
Lying down thumping his tail on the floor	I'm happy
Emitting a continuous, low growl	I'm warning you that I might attack
Teeth bared and snarling	I'm about to attack
Cocking his head to one side	Hmm, that's interesting

How To Toss A Caber

The caber toss is a famous part of the Highland Games in Scotland. A caber is the trunk of a pine tree, with one end thinner than the other. As you might imagine it is very, very heavy. Contestants in this event lift up the huge cabers and toss them into the air, so that they turn over in mid-air, and land on their fatter end before falling flat.

In order to win, a contestant needs to get his caber to land in the twelve o'clock position from the place he threw it. It's all about accuracy, not distance.

Try It Yourself

A full-sized caber is too much, so try a 'broom-handle toss' instead. See who out of your friends can get their 'caber' to land straightest. Here's a step-by-step guide.

1. Take your broom handle (or a pole of a similar size) to a wide open space, and check that there is no one about who might get whacked by a flying caber.

2. Bend down and lean the caber against your shoulder so that it is standing upright. Then lift it off the ground.

3. Move your hands to the bottom and clasp them, palm upwards, around the base of the caber.

4. Move the caber up to about elbow height, and keep the weight balanced against your shoulder. Now you are in the throwing position.

5. Take a short run-up, gaining momentum slowly.

6. Throw your caber upwards and forwards slightly by jerking your clasped hands sharply upwards.

7. The caber should follow a path as shown, landing the other way up. Its end should hit the ground as it stands upright before falling flat.

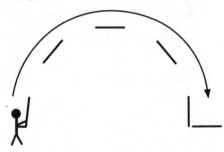

How To Make A Cowpat Float

L ike ice cream? Like cola? Well, there's an easy way to double your enjoyment by making your very own 'cowpat' float.

You Will Need:
- cola
- chocolate ice cream
- a spoon
- a straw
- an ice-cold glass.

What You Do

1. Pour cold water over the outside of a large glass, then put it straight into the freezer. Leave it for around 15 minutes until the thin layer of water on the outside of the glass freezes.

2. Take the glass out of the freezer and add two scoops of the chocolate ice cream.

3. Pour cola slowly into the glass. It will fizz and rise, so don't rush it. (If the bubbles start to overflow, place your index finger on the rim of the glass to burst them.)

4. Grab your spoon and tuck in. Use your straw to reach the cola at the bottom of the glass.

HOW TO GET RID OF HICCUPS

You could gulp down a glass of water, swallow a teaspoon of sugar, eat a piece of dry bread slowly, or gargle water. Alternatively, drink water from the farthest side of the glass rim or hold your breath and count backwards.

Or you could try all these at once – you'll probably feel so ill and confused that you'll forget about your hiccups.

How To Ride A Camel

Camels may not be a common sight in places such as Western Europe and the USA, but in other parts of the world they have been used for hundreds of years to carry goods and people.

Camels' long strides and strong backs make riding them fast and fun. They can reach speeds of up to 60 kilometres per hour. Camel-racing is hugely popular in Australia and the Middle East.

If you're ever given the chance to hop on board one of these one- or two-humped creatures, here's what you should know.

Find A Suitable Camel

Don't even think about trying to ride an untrained camel unless you're prepared to visit a hospital. Find a domesticated camel, with a trained handler.

> Camels have a reputation for being grumpy creatures, so make sure you pick one that's in a good mood!

Make sure the camel has already been raked to remove
any grit, stones or burs that would scratch if you mounted
it. If not, rake the camel with a garden rake.

The saddle is secured with straps so that it is flexible
enough to move with the camel's motion without slipping
off altogether. Ask the handler to check that the saddle
has been fastened securely and will not fall off when you
hop aboard.

Getting On Board

Unless you have a raised platform, the camel will have to kneel or lie down for you to clamber on. Ask the handler to rest one foot on the camel's front leg to make sure that the camel does not get up before you are ready.

Put one foot in one of the stirrups then throw your other leg over the saddle. Try to do this with confidence to show your camel you mean business.

Settle yourself in the saddle and be prepared for the camel to stand up. Lean back, as the camel will bring its back legs up first. Then lean forwards as its front legs come up.

Steering Your Camel

Like horses, camel-riders use reins to direct their mounts. Unlike horses, however, the reins are usually attached to a peg inside the camel's nose. Hold the reins confidently without tugging or pulling them. Pulling them too hard will be painful and annoy your camel – and you don't want to be riding a cross camel.

To turn right, apply slight pressure on the rein in your right hand. Do the opposite to turn left. Relax the reins when your camel is heading in the right direction, because it will become confused if you maintain constant pressure.

Ask the handler to attach a leading rein to your camel. This can be used to lead and guide it as you learn.

> Your camel will respond better if you aren't nervous and jittery, so relax and enjoy the ride.

Getting In The Swing

Riding a walking camel is surprisingly comfortable. Unlike horses, a camel sways from side to side because it lifts both feet on the same side at the same time when walking forwards. Always move with the sway of the camel – if you fight it you'll have a hard time staying in the saddle.

Dismounting

When you are done, you will need to get your camel to kneel down again so you can dismount. Ask the handler to pull down gently on the leading rein and, at the same time, tap lightly on the camel's front legs with a stick. As the handler does this, you must give the command 'koosh!' which is 'lie down!' in camel language. Your camel should obediently drop to his knees.

Once the camel is kneeling ready for you to get off, stand up in the stirrups and throw one leg back over the hump. Jump down, and don't forget to give the camel a pat.

How To Make A Giant Choc-Chip Cookie

If you are a cookie-lover, then you'll know that the best cookies all have two things in common. First, they have lots of chocolate in, and second, they are very, very big.

So, if you plan to make your own cookie, there's only one type to make – a giant choc-chip cookie. Cookie making – even giant cookie making – is quick and easy. Follow these instructions and you'll be munching away in no time.

Warning. When using a hot oven, always use oven gloves and ask an adult to help you.

You Will Need:

- 200g butter
- 135g caster sugar
- 150g brown sugar
- 1 teaspoon vanilla essence
- 2 eggs
- 250g plain flour
- ½ teaspoon baking powder
- ½ teaspoon salt
- 150g chocolate chips
- a large cake tin or baking tray with raised sides.

What You Do

1. Preheat the oven to 180°C (Gas Mark 4). Put the butter, caster sugar, brown sugar and vanilla essence into a bowl. Use a wooden spoon to mix this up as well as you can until it's smooth and creamy.

2. Add the eggs and mix again.

3. Add the flour, baking powder and salt and mix again. Yes, there is an awful lot of mixing to do in this recipe, but the taste of the cookie will make up for tired arms.

4. Next, add your chocolate chips and mix.

5. Grease the bottom of your cake tin or baking tray with butter, and spread the mixture evenly over it to make your giant cookie shape. Don't worry if it's not perfectly round, it will still be delicious.

6. Bake the cookie for 30 minutes, or until golden brown and firm to the touch. All ovens are slightly different so keep an eye on the cookie to make sure it doesn't burn.

If you are using a cake tin, your cookie will rise slightly in the oven, so when it is finished it will look like a cross between a cake and a cookie – what a tasty mix!

7. Leave the cookie to cool and then share it with your friends.

HOW TO BEAT A GORGON

The Gorgons are three mythical creatures named 'Stheno', 'Euryale' and 'Medusa'. These legendary beasts are sisters and all three are incredibly ugly. They have big heads, huge, scary mouths with long tongues hanging out, tusks, and even beards. They also have wings sprouting from their backs, and sharp claws on their hands and feet. Medusa, the most famous of the three, is even worse as her hair is made of live snakes, which hiss and writhe around on her head.

The Gorgons are extremely dangerous creatures to come across, because they have the power to turn anyone who looks at their faces to stone. All around the entrance of the cave where they live there are the frozen, stone bodies of men and animals who have been unfortunate enough to gaze into a Gorgon's face.

Should you come across one of these fearsome creatures, you need to know what to do. To defeat a Gorgon, you need a mirror, a hairbrush and some very dark sunglasses. Wearing your sunglasses, carefully approach the Gorgon. Tell her she needs to brush her hair as it's a mess, and then hand her the brush and mirror. When she sees her reflection in the mirror, she will turn herself to stone.

The only problem you will then have is what to do with her next. Stone Gorgons make excellent garden ornaments. When you have defeated her, why not paint your Gorgon in nice bright colours and put her by your front door? If you have a pond, you could stand her next to this with a fishing rod in her hand and tell everyone she's a very ugly garden gnome!

How To Do The Perfect Press-Up

Press-ups are the perfect exercise. You can do them anywhere, even if you have only got a couple of minutes to spare, you don't need any equipment, and they are excellent for building your strength.

However, they are only the perfect exercise if you have a perfect technique. It is much better to do a few press-ups and perform them correctly, than to do a lot but carry them out the wrong way. Here's how to make sure you get maximum benefit from the exercise:

1. Lie face down on the floor.

2. Place your hands underneath your shoulders with the palms touching the floor and fingers facing forwards.

3. Keep your feet together and position them so it is your toes, not the tops of your feet, that touch the ground.

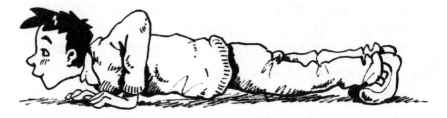

4. Push yourself off the ground by pushing up with your arms until they are straight.

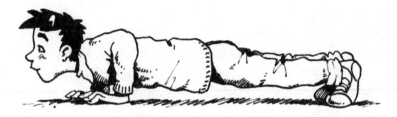

5. Lower yourself slowly by bending your arms at the elbow until your chest hovers just above the floor.

The golden rule of press-ups is to keep your body straight. This takes practice, and you need to concentrate to make sure you do not stick your bottom up in the air or arch your back upwards. Practise in front of a mirror so you can make sure you are in the correct position.

As with all exercise, it's important not to overdo it. Practise your technique by doing a few each day and then build up the number you do slowly.

How To Fake A Scar

Want to convince your friends you have a terrible scar, or simply need to look the part for a Halloween party? Follow these instructions to make a realistic-looking, gruesome, gaping wound. It will require some practice, but it is well worth the effort.

You Will Need:
- make-up – red blusher and foundation that matches your skin tone
- make-up brushes
- make-up remover
- a sachet of unflavoured gelatin
- a lolly stick
- red food colouring
- a tablespoon cornflour
- cotton buds
- a tissue
- a cup of hot water.

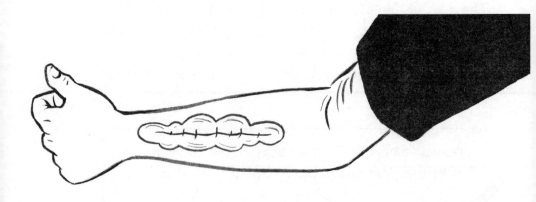

What You Do

1. First, clean the area of skin that you want to create your scar on. It is easiest to practise on your leg, as you will be able to use both your hands. Use make-up remover to get rid of any oil or grease. Pat dry with a tissue.

2. Mix half a cup of hot water with a sachet of unflavoured gelatin. Stir with a lolly stick until the mixture is syrupy. Allow it to cool a little so it won't burn your skin.

3. Now apply a layer of the gelatin syrup to your skin in a rectangle about seven centimetres by five centimetres.

Let this layer dry on your skin, then apply a second layer over the same area.

Don't leave the gelatin in the cup too long as it will set and be too difficult to apply to your skin.

4. Before the second layer of gelatin mix dries, draw the lolly stick across the middle of the layer to create a 'gash' down the centre. Allow this to dry.

You may need to experiment, varying the depth and texture of the gelatin, to achieve a realistic-looking gash.

5. Once the mixture has set, your wound is in place and it's time to cover it with make-up so that its colour blends with your skin. Gently pat some foundation on the 'scar' and blend it all over the scar area. Be as gentle as you can so as not to dent or flatten the gelatin.

6. Now you need to apply some red blusher with a small make-up brush to make the inside of the gash appear pink and sore.

7. Create some fake blood by mixing a few drops of red food colouring with cornflour and a tablespoon of water. Use a cotton bud to dab the 'blood' at various points around the scar. Leave it to dry.

8. Stand back and admire your handiwork. Be prepared to lap up all the sympathy you will receive for your terrible injury.

It's a good idea to ask before you borrow anyone's make-up or you may end up with a scar for real!

How To Play The Toilet Roll

A kazoo is one of the world's simplest musical instruments. Here's how to make one:

You Will Need:
- a cardboard tube (from a roll of kitchen paper, clingfilm, foil or toilet roll)
- greaseproof paper
- an elastic band
- scissors
- a ruler
- a pencil
- coloured pens or paint.

1. Start by decorating your tube (this is optional, but who wants to be seen playing a toilet roll?).

2. That done, cut a square, 12 x 12 centimetres, of greaseproof paper.

3. Place the greaseproof paper over one end of the tube and secure it with the elastic band.

4. Hum or sing into the open end. The greaseproof paper vibrates to give a buzzing effect that enhances the sound you make.

How To Eat Witchetty Grubs

The witchetty grub is a particularly 'delicious' type of moth larva found in the Australian bush and is sometimes eaten by the Aboriginal people who live there.

Here are two ways to enjoy tucking in to a witchetty grub:

Raw
Lower the wriggling beastie into your mouth. Bite it at the neck and start chewing as quickly as you can. Raw witchetty grubs taste like nutty-flavoured cream once you bite into them. Delicious.

Grub Soup
Take the heads off your grubs. Fry a handful of grubs in some cooking oil until their skins are crispy. Add some chopped onions, salt and pepper. Pour in half a litre of chicken stock and cook for half an hour. Cooked witchetty grubs taste like a cross between roast chicken and scrambled eggs.

Top Tip. If you can't get hold of any witchetty grubs, simply replace them with prawns when making your soup.

Prepare each prawn by pulling the head and legs off and peeling the skin away. You don't need to tell your friends you have used prawns, though.

> **Warning.** It is a good idea to stick with prawns, as it is essential to know exactly what bug you are eating and that it is safe to eat, and not the larva of a protected species.

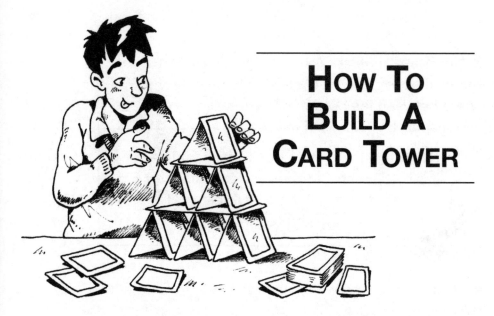

How To Build A Card Tower

There's nothing as stressful as spending a lot of time building a card tower only to make one wrong move and see it collapse. But when you get it right, it's fantastic and very rewarding. So, try to stay cool as you follow these instructions:

1. Take a set of playing cards. Take out two cards and stand them up, leaning them against each other in an upside-down-V-shape that looks a bit like a tent. They should be about the same width apart at the bottom as your middle three fingers. Try building your card tower on carpet as it gives more friction and the cards will be less likely to fall down.

2. Next, take another two cards and build another tent shape, next to the first. There should be only one finger space between the bottom of each of the two shapes. Be careful – if the second shape collapses, it might also knock down your first shape.

3. Once your two tent shapes are standing, lay another card on top of the shapes, resting on the points.

4. Next, make another tent shape on top of the other two by using the card you have just laid as the base. If you have got this far, you are doing very well.

5. Back at ground level, put another tent shape next to the first two.

6. Lay a card across the top, so that it rests on the points of the second and third tent shapes.

7. Use this as the base to build a second tent shape on the second row.

8. Lay a card across the top of the tent shapes on the second row.

9. Finally, place the last tent shape on top of this card. You now have a three-row tower with three tent shapes on the bottom row, two on the middle row and one on the top.

HOW TO BEAT A LIE-DETECTOR TEST

No good spy would ever give anything away. If you ever find yourself captured by enemy agents, you need to keep your secrets closely guarded, especially if you are wired up to a lie-detector machine.

A lie detector measures the body's reactions – heart rate, breathing and sweating. The interrogator will first ask you some simple questions, such as your name.

Look calm, but stay scared, throughout.

He will then ask you a question that he knows you will probably answer with a lie. Throughout, he watches what happens to your heart rate, breathing and sweating when you tell the truth and when you are lying. The differences in these reactions will help him to spot your lies.

Your job is to confuse the lie detector. The trick is to scare yourself. Think of whatever terrifies you the most – for instance rats, spiders, or heights – during all the questions. By increasing your stress level for all answers – true or false – you will confuse the machine so it cannot give an accurate reading.

HOW TO SPEAK IN CODE

- **Eggy-Peggy.** Add 'egg' before each vowel.
  Example: 'Eggi eggam thegge beggest.' ('I am the best.')

- **Gree.** Add 'gree' to the end of every word.
  Example: 'Igree amgree thegree bestgree.'

- **Na.** Add 'na' to the end of every word.
  Example: 'Ina amna thena bestna.'

- **Pig Latin.** Move the first letter to the end of the word and add 'ay' to it.
  Example: 'Iay maay hetay estbay.'

How To Save A Penalty

You're in goal and a penalty is awarded against your team. Don't panic. If you don't save the penalty, everyone will understand, but if you do – you're a hero. Here's how you can become a team legend.

▸ The rules say you are not allowed to move off the goal line before the ball is struck by the person taking the penalty. So jump up and down on the spot with your arms and legs spread wide apart. This will make you as big a target as possible and hopefully put the striker off.

▸ Watch the striker's body language as he prepares to take the shot. Look carefully to see if his eyes give away which corner of the goal he intends to aim the ball at.

▸ Watch to see if the striker is nervous or confident. If he is nervous he is likely to hesitate or make a weak shot. If he is confident he will probably try to show off by hitting it over your head. If you know it's coming, get ready to jump high to save the ball.

- If the striker is right-footed, he is likely to strike the right side of the ball. This will mean the ball will be aimed towards the centre of the net or to the left-hand side, so aim your dive accordingly.

- Always, always dive. Even if the ball is blasted down the middle, you may save it with your legs or feet. Dive just before the ball is struck. It will be travelling so fast that if you dive after the ball is hit, it will be in the net before you have any chance of making a save.

With a bit of luck you will leave the pitch as the 'Man of the Match'!

HOW TO MAKE A BALLOON CHANGE COLOUR

What happens when you stick a pin into a balloon? There's a loud, 'Pop!' and you're left with the shreds of a burst balloon. Right? Not any more. Find out how to wow people by popping a balloon and have it magically change colour.

You Will Need:
- a red balloon
- a blue balloon
- sticky tape
- a pencil
- a pin.

What You Do

1. Put a double-sided loop of sticky tape on the biggest part of your blue balloon.

2. Slide a pencil into the neck of the blue balloon and use this to help you push it inside the red one. You may have to work the red balloon down the pencil bit by bit. When you've finished, remove the pencil carefully.

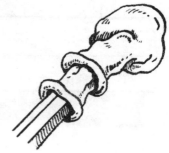

3. Blow up the blue balloon (this will blow up the red one as well), and tie a knot in the bottom.

4. Stand in front of your audience holding the balloons. All they will see is the red balloon on the outside.

5. Find where the sticky tape is, by looking through the red balloon, and then jab it with a pin at this point.

The red balloon will burst with a loud bang and you will be left holding the blue balloon. To anybody watching, it looks as if the red balloon has suddenly, magically changed colour.

How To Flip A Pancake

If you fancy a nice, quick snack, have a go at making a delicious pancake. This recipe is enough to make eight pancakes, so you can share them with your friends.

You Will Need:
- 125g plain flour
- 250ml milk
- an egg

- olive oil
- a tasty topping
- a fantastic flipping technique.

What You Do

1. Add the flour and milk to a mixing bowl.

2. Crack the egg and pour this into the bowl. Now mix the ingredients together with a whisk until the mixture (called 'batter') is smooth and has no lumps.

3. Heat about a teaspoonful of oil in a frying pan and then tilt the pan and move it in a circular motion so a thin layer of oil covers the bottom of the pan.

4. Using a ladle, pour a small amount of batter into the middle of the pan. Repeat the motion you made with the oil to spread a thin layer of batter over the whole pan.

5. Cook the pancake on a low-to-medium heat until the batter is firm.

Flipping Marvellous

▸ Shake the frying pan to make sure the pancake is loose. If it's sticking to the pan, ease it up gently with a spatula. The pancake needs to be loose so you get a good takeoff.

▸ Hold the pan loosely in your hand. Give it a quick, sharp flick upwards. Start with the pan pointing slightly downwards and use a scooping motion to make sure the pancake turns over in the air.

▸ Catch the pancake in your frying pan and let it cook for a minute on the other side.

Top Topping Tips

Here are some tasty topping ideas to get you started:

- lemon and sugar
- maple syrup
- fruit and ice cream
- ham and cheese
- tomato and mushroom.

How To 'Pop-Up' On A Surfboard

The key to standing up successfully on a surfboard is learning the 'pop-up' manoeuvre. This is the basic move that helps you get to your feet on your board as quickly and smoothly as possible.

The best place to practise 'popping-up' on your surfboard is on dry land. Learning on an unstable surface like a floating surfboard is only likely to take you in one direction – under the water. So, instead of risking constant dunkings, practise on dry land. Take your surfboard, remove the fins (which are usually detachable) and lie it flat on the beach, on the grass in your garden or even on the floor of your bedroom.

What You Do
1. Lie flat on your board. Begin by doing a press-up – pushing your body upwards by straightening your arms.

2. Once your arms are straight, jump your legs and feet forwards, bringing your knees towards your chest, so you are in a crouching position. If you are right-handed, your right foot should be slightly in front of your left foot.

3. Straighten your legs so you are standing in a sideways position with your feet apart. Your right foot should be near the middle of the board, the other towards the tail.

Well done, you've mastered stage one of surfing. Keep going!

How To Catch A Wave

Before you can impress everyone with your smooth surfing skills, you need to learn how to catch a wave. Grab your board and follow the steps below – you'll soon be catching waves all the way in to shore.

What You Do

1. When you are waist-deep in the water, lie face down on your board and start paddling out to sea. As you reach the point where waves are breaking, shift your weight forwards to lower the front of your board and paddle fast, ducking under the breaking waves. This is called 'duck-diving'. You are aiming to pass the place where the waves are breaking to where they are starting to form a swell.

2. Once you're in position, stop paddling and sit astride your board slightly nearer the back than the front. Wait until you spot a wave that is big enough or travelling fast enough to pick you up and carry you all the way to shore.

3. As the wave approaches, turn and point your board towards the shore. Lie flat and start to paddle. Don't let your body get too close to the nose of your board as you may push it underwater. As you feel the wave lifting and pushing you towards the shore, paddle as fast as you can.

4. As the wave carries you forward, stop paddling. To keep your board moving as fast as possible, raise your chest a little to shift your weight backwards. However, do not lean back too far, as this will slow you down.

5. Once you've caught a few waves, you're ready to begin standing up on your surfboard using the pop-up move you learnt on pages 126 and 127.

Warnings

▸ Only go in the sea if you can see a red and yellow flag flying on the beach – this means there is a trained lifeguard on the beach and it is safe to swim. Keep to the area between the flags.

▸ Always make sure you stay out of the way of other surfers if the water is busy. They will not be pleased if you cut in on their wave.

▸ Never go surfing alone, and be sure to return to the beach before it gets dark.

▸ Don't go into the water if you see 'No swimming' signs, a red flag or a warning of strong currents.

How To Ride A Wave

Once you've mastered catching waves and popping-up on your surfboard, you need to learn how to ride a wave.

Surfing standing up is all about riding along the front of a wave, staying parallel to the beach. This allows you to surf faster and for longer.

It takes a lot of practice, but here are some top tips.

▸ Once the wave has begun to carry you forwards, pop-up to get you on your feet.

▸ To keep going as fast as possible, you need to travel along the unbroken part of a wave (not the whitewater). To do this you will need to steer your board in the right direction. Begin by keeping your body low – bending your legs and adopting a crouching stance. Position your front foot in the direction you want to travel and lean your weight slightly on to this foot.

▸ Try to keep most of your body weight over the middle of the board – this will help stop you from falling off.

▸ Focus your eyes on the part of the wave you want to ride.

▸ You're surfing!

Watch out you don't wipeout – but if you do, just get back on that board and give it another go.

HOW TO SHINE ON PARADE

Parade-ground sergeants have a real thing about shiny boots. So here's how to get a 'spit and shine' polish. This is called a 'spit and shine' polish, because a lot of soldiers don't bother using water. They just spit on the cloth instead.

You Will Need:
- a pair of leather boots
- two soft cloths
- shoe polish
- water.

Time To Shine

1. Put one hand inside the boot and, with the other hand, use a cloth to spread plenty of polish over your boot. Then leave it to dry for at least five minutes.

2. Wrap the cloth around your index finger (the one next to your thumb) and dip your finger and the cloth in water.

3. Rub the boot with the damp cloth. Do this by making your finger go round and round in small circles. After a while, the polish on it will start to shine.

4. Dip your finger and the cloth into the polish again and apply another thin layer of polish to the boot. Don't use much polish this time. Use the same circular motion as before and keep rubbing until the boot shines even more.

5. Repeat this two or three more times until the boot is highly polished, then use a clean, dry cloth to give a final shine.

6. Check to make sure you can see your face reflected in the polish and, if so, you are ready to go on parade.

HOW TO RECEIVE YOUR KNIGHTHOOD

You kneel on the ground with your head bowed as the person before you clutches a sharp, steel sword. The room is silent as you wait for the weapon to fall.

Sounds terrifying, doesn't it? Believe it or not, this could actually be the greatest moment of your life – the day you receive your knighthood. If it is, then the person raising the sword is none other than the Queen of the United Kingdom herself and, in a few moments, you are about to become a genuine knight.

Knighthoods are awarded for great achievements and have been presented to artists, musicians, actors, sports stars, charity fundraisers and others who have performed their job outstandingly well.

It's Knight Time

The day of your knighthood is called your 'investiture'. It is a very grand, formal occasion and it is important that you know how to behave.

You will be led into the ballroom and will stand with the other people waiting to receive their honour. Once everyone is in place, the Queen will enter the room

escorted by two soldiers. The Yeomen of the Guard, who are the Queen's bodyguards, will also be there.

The national anthem, 'God Save the Queen', is then played, after which a lord calls the name of each person and states the reason they are being knighted.

I Dub Thee ...

When your name is called, step forward and kneel in front of the Queen. She will place her sword blade on your right shoulder and then on your left shoulder. This is called 'dubbing' and, as she places the blade on your shoulders, she will say, 'I dub thee Sir (your name).'

Congratulations! You are now a knight. This means you can put 'Sir' in front of your name on letters and emails, and can insist everyone calls you 'Sir', even your parents.

How To Go Crabbing

Crabbing's a great thing to do if you're on holiday by the sea or a tidal river. It's easy to master and you can normally catch crabs without a lot of specialist knowledge or fancy equipment.

You Will Need:
- a piece of string or fishing line
- a metal hook (the top of a wire coat hanger would work)
- a nut or bolt
- some uncooked bacon to use as bait
- a bucket
- a small fishing net.

What You Do

1. To make your crabbing line, tie the hook to the end of your string or fishing line. Tie the nut or bolt to the line directly above the hook to weigh the line down.

2. Find a good spot – beside a harbour wall, bridge, floating jetty or pontoon. There are usually plenty of crabs to go round, so you don't need to find an isolated spot.

3. Fill your bucket with water from the sea or tidal river – you can put some bacon in it if you have some spare.

4. Bait the hook on the end of your crabbing line with some bacon. (Wash your hands after handling the bait.)

5. Drop your baited hook into the water and let it sink to the bottom, keeping a tight hold of your end of the line. Wait for a few moments for your weight to settle on the bottom.

6. Wait patiently until you feel a slight tug on the line. Then bring your line up slowly until you can see if anything is on the end. If you've been successful, it will have a crab clinging on to it. Reach down with your fishing net and transfer the crab from the hook into your bucket of water.

Warning. Remember that crabs are living, feeling creatures. You should always treat them gently and lower them back to where they came from once you have caught them. Don't throw them back as this might hurt them, and don't leave them on the shore where birds may eat them.

How To Survive At Sea

You're cruising at a rate of knots when suddenly your boat begins to sink. The gently-lapping sea instantly becomes a treacherous ocean. In order to survive you will need skill, endurance, luck – and the following tips.

Stay On Board
Don't rush to abandon ship. Even if your boat is damaged, you're almost certainly better off on board. Why? Because the bigger the boat, the more visible it will be to a rescue party, and the better protected you are from the wind, water and sun.

Proper Provisions
If you have to leave your boat because it sinks, then your life raft should be equipped with a basic survival kit. This will include a short-wave radio, a GPS receiver (a Global Positioning System receiver which can calculate your exact position in the ocean), a compass, a knife, self-igniting flares, a waterproof watch, a waterproof torch, warm blankets, a box of matches in a waterproof container, a first-aid kit and some dry food.

However, the most important thing you should have on board is fresh water. A lack of fresh water will dramatically reduce the number of days you can stay alive.

Warning. No matter how thirsty you get, NEVER drink seawater. It is three times as salty as your blood and your body would not be able to cope. It would also make you extremely thirsty.

You will also need to eat. There should be provisions in your raft, but once these are used up, don't panic. Fish should be plentiful in the ocean and flying fish may even land in your raft. If you don't have a fishing rod then try using twine and hooks made from wire or aluminium cans.

You can eat the flesh of fish raw. Don't forget to eat the eyes as well. Gross, but these contain water, too. Make sure you don't eat the organs or you may become sick.

Stay Dry

Seawater is your number one enemy, so your main aim should be to keep dry and stay warm. If you are out in cold weather, you could develop 'hypothermia' (a condition that sets in when your body temperature drops below its normal level). This can kill within a very short space of time. If you're adrift in hot weather, exposure to seawater and sun can damage your skin, leading to blisters and other infections.

So if your life raft has a canopy, use it. If not, try to rig up sheets and blankets as a shelter from the waves and from the sun as soon as possible. If you remain exposed, you will survive for a shorter time than if you are under cover.

Stay Or Go?

Even if you know your location, trying to row towards land may not be a good idea. Currents and riptides may push you further from your destination and your rowing efforts may waste precious energy.

If your boat was able to send a distress signal before it sank, staying close to where you sent the flare will mean that you are more likely to be found by potential rescuers.

Signal And Survive

A survivor in a life raft will be almost invisible in the vast seascape. As a result, it's vital you are ready to signal to any passing plane or ship. If you have self-igniting flares and a short-wave radio then make sure you know how to use them so you are ready to swing into action.

If you don't have either device, use a hand-held mirror to reflect sunlight towards rescuers, or attract attention by using a whistle or a torch. As a last resort, waving brightly-coloured material may also be effective.

> **Warning.** Before setting out on a voyage, always tell someone your route and the time you will arrive at your destination. This way people will know where to look if you don't arrive.

How To Navigate By The Stars

The night sky above you is full of twinkling stars. Did you know that these stars work as a giant compass? Because the stars' positions relating to each other always stay the same, people can use them to find their way in the dark. Sailors out on the open sea often use the stars to plot a course and steer their ships.

Super Stargazing

The way to do this is to find Polaris, which is also called the North Star, as it is almost directly above the North Pole. Polaris helps you find north. Once you know which way is north, you can also find east, south and west.

It takes a little bit of time to become skilled at finding stars, so practise every time there is a clear night, and soon you'll be a night-sky navigator.

How To Find North

1. To help identify stars, they are put into groups called 'constellations'. The group of stars you need to find in the sky is part of the constellation Ursa Major, and is called the Big Dipper.

2. Look at the two stars at the right of the Big Dipper. These are called the 'pointer' stars. Now imagine a line drawn between these two stars and continue this line upwards. This line leads you to another, very bright, star. This is Polaris, the North Star.

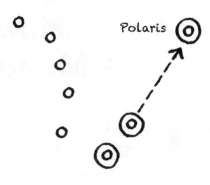

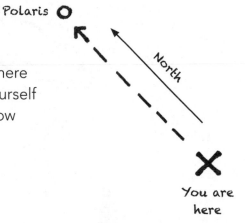

3. So, to work out which direction north is from where you are standing, turn yourself to face Polaris. You are now facing north.

In the southern hemisphere (the part of the Earth that is below the equator), Polaris cannot be seen. Instead, people in the southern hemisphere use a constellation called Crux (also called the Southern Cross) to help them find south.

How To Be
A Memory Master

If you've been getting dates wrong in your history tests, forgetting to record your favourite TV programme, or if your puppy is starving because you forgot to buy his biscuits – don't worry. Here are some ways to turn yourself into a memory master.

Practice Makes Perfect

Play this game with your friends to keep your memory in peak condition. Before your friends arrive, collect 20 objects and put them on a table. Here are some suggestions:

- a pencil
- a plastic toy
- a DVD
- a mug
- a sock
- a fishing rod
- an ice cream cone
- a mobile phone
- a stone
- a key

- a paper clip
- a baseball cap
- a book
- a spoon
- an apple
- a sugar cube
- scissors
- a ruler
- a watch
- a yo-yo.

Now cover all the objects with a cloth. When your friends are gathered round, lift the cloth for 20 seconds. Then cover the table again and get everyone to write down every object they can remember. The person who remembers the most wins.

Memory Techniques

Here are some tips to help you remember things:

▸ Rhymes and memorable sentences are great ways to make remembering information easier. Here's a useful way to remember the names of all the planets and their order in the solar system, starting with the nearest to the Sun. (In case you were wondering, Pluto is no longer officially a planet.)

My Very Educated Mother Just Served Us Noodles.

The first letter of each word in this sentence is the same as the first letter of each of the planets:

Mercury, Venus, Earth, Mars, Jupiter, Saturn, Uranus, Neptune.

▸ Try to make memorable mental pictures of things you need to remember.

For example, if you keep forgetting to feed a pet, imagine it doing something crazy like nibbling the roof of your house. This visual image will pop into your mind, triggering your memory.

▸ Try making up sentences for things you need to remember. Ever wondered why you can remember your team's results but not the name of some old king? It is the joy (and misery) that you experience following your team that makes it easier to remember their triumphs (and defeats).

Try to attach some emotion to the information that you need to remember by finding out some more interesting details – for example, Prince Albert died of typhoid in 1861. His widow, Queen Victoria, wore black every day until her own death forty years later. By knowing that fact, you will be far more likely to remember the date of his death.

HOW TO BE A KUNG-FU KING

One of the most famous moves in kung fu is the 'High Kick'. Practise in front of a mirror or try kicking a cushion suspended at chest height. This will allow you to improve the speed, power and accuracy of your kick.

Here's how you can sharpen your kicking skills in this vital area:

1. Stand at a 45° angle to your target. Position the leg you are going to kick with just behind your hips and the other leg just in front. Seventy per cent of your weight should be resting on your back leg.

2. Transfer your weight forward on to your front foot, keeping your back as straight as possible. As you do, lift your kicking leg with the knee bent. Pivot on your front foot so your raised knee is pointing directly at your target. Lift the knee as high as you can (at least as high as your waist).

3. You are aiming to hit your target with the top part of your foot. Do this by straightening your leg rapidly in a kicking motion.

4. Once you have made contact, quickly return to your starting position.

> **Warning.** Never aim a High Kick at anyone, except in self-defence.

HOW TO BE A BODYGUARD

Being a bodyguard is a job that involves danger and excitement, and requires constant vigilance. If that sounds tempting, and you want to become a bodyguard that no one will mess with, follow these instructions.

1. Look around you constantly. Danger can come from anywhere, at any time.

2. Bodyguards are usually very tall and extremely muscly and strong. Do lots of press-ups and eat lots of protein to make yourself as big and brawny as you can.

3. Always chew gum – bodyguards need to look tough and cool to impress the person they are guarding, and to intimidate everyone else. Wear sunglasses for the same reason, and keep your face set in a mean and moody expression.

4. If you are guarding a celebrity, stop them being mobbed by large groups of their fans. Do this as peacefully as you can.

5. If anything happens, get whoever you are protecting away as quickly as possible. Always plan an escape route, wherever you are.

6. Remember your job is to protect the good guy, not catch the bad guy. If someone attacks and then runs away, don't chase after him, stay with the person you are protecting.

How To Make A Magic Cup Of Coffee

Here's how to perform a trick that will convince your audience you have a bottomless cup of coffee.

You Will Need:
- a full cup of coffee and a saucer
- 2 sugar cubes
- a gullible friend.

What You Do
1. Hold the cup and saucer in your left hand. Hold one sugar cube clearly in your right hand and conceal the other cube under the saucer in your left hand.

2. Tip the cup and saucer very slightly towards your audience. This will ensure that the hidden sugar cube is completely concealed under the saucer.

3. Drop the cube in your right hand into the cup of coffee. The instant the sugar cube hits the bottom of the cup, drop the sugar cube out of your left hand on to the floor.

It's all about timing, so practise until you can make it look as if one sugar cube is falling through a bottomless coffee cup.

HOW TO BECOME A ROCK 'N' ROLL DRUMMING LEGEND

The drums are great fun to play but it takes practice and skill to master playing them. Here are some simple exercises to set you on the path to rock-and-roll-stardom.

1. Pat yourself on the top of your head with an up and down movement, while using your other hand to rub your stomach in circles. Not easy, is it? Drumming is all about doing different things with different parts of your body, and it takes quite a while to be able to do this well.

The next exercise is harder. See how well you do.

2. Tap a finger of your left hand on the table with a regular rhythm. Every other time it hits the table, hit the table at the same time with a finger of your right hand. The rhythm should go: Left … Left and Right … Left … Left and Right … Left ….

3. Got the hang of it? Excellent. Now, repeat the exercise, but every fourth beat, stamp on the floor with your right foot. The rhythm should now go: Left … Left and Right … Left … Left and Right and Right Foot … and so on.

If you have managed to get this far, you're doing great. Don't relax just yet, though. There is one more step.

4. Repeat the exercise, but on the second beat and every four beats after that, stamp on the floor with your left foot. The final, complete rhythm should now go:

Left Hand
Left Hand, Right Hand, Left Foot
Left Hand
Left Hand, Right Hand, Right Foot.
Left Hand
Left Hand, Right Hand, Left Foot
Left Hand
Left Hand, Right Hand, Right Foot.

If you've got this far successfully, you've really got the beat! Take some lessons, start saving for a drum kit, grow your hair and get drumming!

How To Be A Superstar Charity Fundraiser

Raising money for charity is great, but with so many good causes around, you need to work to get noticed.

Careful Planning

Your first task is to decide what to raise money for. This could be a local organization, medical research or helping people in poorer countries.

Next, decide how to raise the money. One of the best ways is through sponsorship, where people pay you to complete an activity.

If you decide on a sponsored event, you need to choose what it will be. Fundraising is more effective and much more fun if you do it with friends, so why not organize a sponsored swim at your local pool, for instance?

Organizing The Swim

Before you start, ask permission from the pool's manager, and make sure that a lifeguard can be present at all times during the swimming event. Ask an adult to help out with the organizing, and oversee your swim.

Set Your Sponsorship Target

The more challenging it is, the more likely people are to give you money. For example, you could do a five kilometre swim. Don't worry if you can't swim this far, you can make it a team effort.

Design sponsorship forms, so that everyone taking part can ask people to sponsor them. The forms should include details of the event, a column for people's names and a column for the amount of money they are giving.

Give all the swimmers an information sheet for the day with the time, date and meeting place. It should also include what people need to bring with them (such as a swimming costume, towel and snacks), and a swimming rota so everyone understands how the day will work.

Once you've finished and had a well-earned rest, you and your friends need to collect the money and decide how you will give it to the organization you are supporting. You may be able to deliver it in person to a local representative, or you might need to send it to the organization. Ask an adult to help you with this.

How To Be A Frothing-Foam Fighter

Water fights are fantastically wet fun, but imagine a foam fight that ensures everyone gets the frothiest of soakings.

You Will Need:
- a lot of space (preferably a garden or a park)
- some large plastic bottles (lids removed)
- washing-up liquid
- baking soda
- vinegar
- warm water.

1. Add a good squeeze of washing-up liquid to your plastic bottle. Then fill it three-quarters full with warm water. Add two teaspoons of baking soda.

2. Put your hand over the top of the bottle and give it a good shake so the liquid starts bubbling up. (Never screw on the lid as this can be dangerous – and explosive!)

3. Add a final magic ingredient – a teaspoon of vinegar. The bubble mixture in each bottle should magically turn to foam.

4. Squeeze your bottle to shoot out the foam. Take aim and let the foam fight begin.

> **Warning.** Avoid squirting foam in your opponent's eyes at all times.

How To Fly A Kite

It flies, it soars, it dives, and you are in control. Kites are fantastic fun, can be flown wherever there's open space, and they are easy to fly. Grab a friend, follow these instructions and your kite will soon be high in the air.

High Flyer

1. For your kite to fly, you need wind. It doesn't have to be a strong wind, but a decent breeze is essential.

2. Face into the oncoming wind, then turn your back on it.

3. Keep hold of the spool of string. Ask your partner to take the kite and walk at least 15 metres away from you and then to stand holding the kite loosely in his hands. He should walk in the same direction as you are facing.

4. Pull the string so it is tight and wait for a good gust of wind.

5. Ask your partner to hold the kite above his head, then pull on the string so that the kite leaves your partner's hands and rises in the air.

6. Once your kite is flying, you can gradually unwind your spool to let out more string so the kite can climb higher.

7. If the wind drops and the kite starts to fall, wind the string in or run away from the kite to pull the line tight.

8. To land your kite, simply walk towards it while winding in the string.

Don't Fly Your Kite ...

▸ during bad weather

▸ near electric cables, telephone lines or trees

▸ over people, in case it falls on them

▸ near roads.

If you follow these four don'ts, you'll be sure to keep yourself, your kite, and everybody else safe.

How To Stop
A Nosebleed

It can be quite frightening to suddenly discover blood pouring from your nose. Usually, nosebleeds are neither painful nor dangerous, so there's nothing to worry about. If you find yourself with a nosebleed, stay calm, follow the advice below and the bleeding should soon stop.

▸ Most people lean backwards when they find they have a nosebleed. Actually, this is the opposite of what you should do. The blood has to flow, and if you lean backwards it is going to go down your

throat, which won't be very pleasant. If you have a nosebleed, sit somewhere comfortable and lean forwards.

▶ Pinch your nose at the point just above your nostrils. This dams the blood in your nose, and blood that isn't moving forms into a solid clot. You need to pinch your nose for at least ten minutes for this to work.

▶ With your other hand, apply a cold flannel or an ice pack to the side of your nose. Nosebleeds are often caused by the rupturing of tiny blood vessels, and making the area cold will cause these to shrink and the blood will stop flowing.

▶ When you let go, the nosebleed will most likely have stopped. If it hasn't you're going to have to pinch it again, perhaps for longer this time.

▶ When the bleeding has stopped, your nose may feel blocked up and you may want to blow it. Don't. If you blow your nose, you will release the blood clot and the bleeding could start again. Avoid any running around or physical games for the next few hours.

> If the nosebleed doesn't stop after following these instructions, tell your parents and go to the doctors.

How To Pitch A Tent

Nothing beats the feeling of crawling into your tent after a hard day in the great outdoors. Here are some top tips to prepare you for pitching your tent like a pro.

The Perfect Place To Pitch

▶ Look for a spot to put up your tent well before it gets dark. If you're not staying on an official site, ask permission before pitching your tent.

▶ Choose a site that is not in a valley or a ditch. If you choose either of those places and it rains, your tent could flood.

▶ Choose a spot that is sheltered from the wind. If you pitch your tent on an exposed area or on the top of a hill you and your tent may risk being blown away!

▶ Choose somewhere as flat as possible. If there is a slight slope, it's best to make sure you sleep with your head higher than your feet.

▶ Check for any signs of animal tracks or insects. Camping on an ants' nest could result in a serious case of 'ants in your pants'.

Pitching The Tent

Each tent is different – some will pop up by themselves, some require poles and flysheets. You must practise pitching your tent before an expedition. Know how it works, so you can put it up quickly when night is falling.

Never leave home without checking all the pieces of your tent are in the bag and the instructions are packed.

When pegging out the groundsheet of your tent, stretch it out as flat as possible. Use a rubber mallet to bash the metal pegs through the loops. If you have a separate groundsheet, always make sure that it is tucked up inside the tent so that no water can get in.

When your tent is up, peg down the guy ropes so your tent is standing up without any creases. (Guy ropes are the ropes on the outside of the tent.) When you're putting the pegs into the ground, put them in at an angle of 45°, leaning away from the tent. The ropes should pull on them at an angle of 90°.

If it looks like rain, slacken the guy ropes slightly. This will reduce the chance of the pegs being dragged out of the ground or the tent material tearing in a heavy shower.

Striking Your Tent

When it's time to take your tent down – known as 'striking' your tent – always take up the groundsheet first. Turn it upside down to allow it to dry and brush off any grass or mud.

Pull the pegs out of the ground one by one. If you struggle to pull your tent pegs out, tap them backwards and forwards with the mallet to loosen them.

Try and dry your tent before packing it away. If you have to pack it up wet, dry it as soon as possible or it may rot.

Before you leave to go camping, make sure you tell an adult where you are going. Always carry a mobile phone on an expedition so you can let an adult know where you are at all times.

HOW TO READ SOMEONE'S MIND

Mystify your friends, and amaze your enemies with this simple yet effective mindreading trick.

‣ Ask a friend to pick a number between 1 and 5.

‣ Ask them to multiply that number by 9.

‣ Ask them to add the digits of the number they get.

‣ Now ask them to subtract 5 from their answer.

‣ Tell your friend to think of the letter in the alphabet that corresponds to their number (1 is A, 2 is B and so on).

‣ Tell them to think of a country in Europe that starts with that letter. Now ask them to think of an animal that starts with the last letter of that country. And then a colour that starts with the last letter of their animal.

‣ Now tell them that you know what they are thinking, and that it is an orange kangaroo in Denmark.

Chances are that you're right.

How To Train Your Goldfish To Play Football

A lot of people are unkind about goldfish, saying they only remember things for three seconds and that they are not very intelligent. Well, here's how to prove them wrong by teaching your goldfish to be a soccer star.

First, prepare your pitch. Buy green pebbles for the bottom of your goldfish's bowl or tank from your local pet shop. Next, make a simple goal using three small sticks taped together. Don't use a net, though – you don't want your goldfish getting tangled up.

Training

Have you ever noticed that whenever you go near the fish tank, the fish swim to the surface? This is because they know they might be fed when someone comes near the tank. It is this behaviour that will help you train them.

> ▸ Put a small ball in the tank – light enough for the fish to be able to move but heavy enough to sink in the water.

▶ Now, wait. Sooner or later, the fish will nudge the ball. When this happens, give a tiny piece of food to the fish.

▶ Wait until the fish moves the ball again and drop in another piece of food. If you do this often enough, the fish will learn that nudging the ball leads to being fed and will start to move the ball around. You will need to be patient with your fish as it does take time to learn. It will probably take a couple of training sessions a day, for two to three weeks, to turn your goldfish into a footballing legend.

Warning. It is very important not to overfeed the fish. Don't give it more than its usual daily allowance and stop feeding the fish if it doesn't swim up and eat the food immediately.

How To Make A Coin Go Through A Table

Slamming a coin down on a table so that it looks like it goes straight through is a quick and impressive trick to learn. It's also a trick you can do anywhere as all you need is a coin and a table. The best time to do it, though, is at lunch or dinner when everyone is sitting around a table.

What You Do

1. Sit at the table with the coin in your right hand and your left hand resting on your lap.

2. Raise your right hand and slam the coin on the table so your hand is covering it. Slide your hand off the table and make a fist so it looks like you are picking the coin up.

3. When you slide your hand to the edge of the table, let the coin fall into your lap. It is important that you sit with your legs together so the coin doesn't drop on to the floor.

4. Now, raise your right hand, still in a fist. Remember there is no coin in this hand now, although those watching think that there is.

5. While everyone is watching your right hand, pick the coin off your lap with your left hand and hold it under the table at the spot above which your right hand is going to land.

6. Slam your right hand down on the table so that, once again, your hand is flat. At exactly the same time as your right hand lands, use your left hand to hit the underside of the table with the coin. It is this sound of the coin hitting the table that makes the trick work.

7. As everyone watches, raise your right hand so they can see there is no coin on the table or in your hand.

8. Remove your left hand from under the table and show the coin. To the confused audience, it will look as if the coin has gone straight through the table and landed in your left hand.

HOW TO MAKE THE PERFECT SNOWBALL

Making a perfect snowball is easy, right? Wrong. Anyone can create a snowball that falls apart too soon or doesn't fall apart at all, but making one that has maximum explosive effect takes skill and practice.

Perfect Temperature

The perfect time to make snowballs is when the temperature outside is around freezing. If the temperature falls below freezing, the snow gets dry and powdery and won't stick together. If this happens, try looking for snow beside your house that might be a little warmer and wetter.

If the temperature rises above freezing, the snow will be too slushy and wet. Look for snow further away from your house on an exposed area but out of direct sunlight, as this should be colder.

Lower Layers

When you locate a patch of good snow, brush off the top layer of fallen snow and use the lower levels of snow that have been packed together. This is perfect snowball-making snow.

Packing A Snowball

Start by scooping up the snow and bring your cupped hands together. As you start to press the snow together you should be able to hear the squeaking sound of the snow compressing. Don't press too hard, and stop as soon as the ball starts to feel hard. Add one more scoop of snow and press it around the ball you have already made.

Bare Hands Are Best To Make Snowballs

The heat from your body helps warm the snow so that it is easier to mould. Throwing it is the only way to truly test your creation. The perfect snowball should 'explode' on impact, leaving your target (or victim) in a cloud of snow and a tell-tale snowy imprint where the snowball hit.

> **Warning.** Never aim your snowballs at people's faces – this can damage their eyes. Never throw snowballs at moving cars or anywhere near a busy road.

How To Become An Expert

A great way to convince everyone you are very, very clever, and extremely important, is to become an expert called an '-ologist'. There's an -ology for just about everything. Here are a few ideas to get you started:

Palaeontology – Studying fossils.

Archaeology – Studying history by searching for, and digging up, old ruins and objects.

Egyptology – Studying ancient Egypt.

Mythology – Studying myths.

Ecology – Studying the environment and the animals and plants that live in it.

Geology – Studying rocks.

Ornithology – Studying birds.

As you can see, -ologies sound pretty impressive.

Choosing Your Own -Ology

▶ The most impressive -ologies are those that are hard to pronounce. For instance, you could become an 'ichthyologist' (an expert in fish), or a 'vexillologist' (an expert in flags).

▸ Some -ologies are easier to become an expert in than others as you don't need qualifications. For example, 'cryptozoology' is the study of animals that may or may not exist. So, if you go off hunting for the Loch Ness Monster or a Yeti – even if you don't find one – you are a cryptozoologist.

▸ You can, of course, invent your own -ologies. 'Eating-ice-cream-ology' won't impress anyone, but experts have a trick – they use the ancient Latin language to create -ologies. The Latin for 'to have dinner' is 'cenare' and the Latin for 'ice' is 'glacies', so an expert in eating ice cream for dinner could be a 'cenareglaciesologist'. There you have a tasty field of expertise that will make sure everyone is amazed by your intelligence.

How To Draw A Mural

A mural is a large picture painted straight on to a wall. Here's a simple method that will have you drawing a marvellous mural in no time.

You Will Need:
- a picture or photograph
- paintbrushes
- various colours of emulsion paint
- a soft lead pencil
- a sheet of tracing paper
- a ruler
- a wall
- sheets of old newspaper.

What You Do

1. Ask permission before you start your mural. Then find a picture you would like to turn into a mural. It could be a photograph, or your own drawing. Place a sheet of tracing paper over the top of the image to protect it.

2. You are going to draw a grid over it. Using a ruler, draw a pencil line on the tracing paper down the centre of the picture. Then draw a line across the centre of the picture. You now have four boxes, each the same size.

3. Draw a line down the middle of the top left-hand box and across the centre of it. Repeat this for all four boxes, making a grid of 16 equal-sized boxes.

4. Draw a large box on the wall using a soft lead pencil. This box will contain 16 larger boxes. For example, if your picture is 15 centimetres long and 10 centimetres wide, you could draw a box that's 150 centimetres long and 100 centimetres wide.

5. Divide this box into 16 smaller boxes using the same method as before. You now have a larger grid to match the one you drew on your picture.

6. Draw the outline of the mural using the boxes as a guide. Copy the bit of the picture that is in the bottom left box into the bottom left box on the wall, and continue until the outline is complete.

7. Put some old newspapers on the floor so paint doesn't drip on to it, and begin painting your mural masterpiece.

How To Survive In Space

If you're very rich you could go to space for a holiday. In case that happens, or you become an astronaut, here's how to survive in space:

▸ You will need to exercise frequently to minimize the loss of bone and muscle mass caused by weightlessness. Gym equipment is provided.

▸ You will eat in the galley. The food is in containers attached to a tray which is in turn attached either to you or to a wall (otherwise your meal floats off). The meals themselves are not made up of tablets, though – you get proper appetizing food just like at home.

▸ You will sleep in bunk-style sleeping quarters or in sleeping bags. These have to be attached to a wall or they will float about and you'll wake up in another part of the station.

▸ As there's no washing machine aboard, you will need to take with you a great deal of clothing. Dirty clothes are sealed in plastic bags, in much the same way as all the rubbish is.

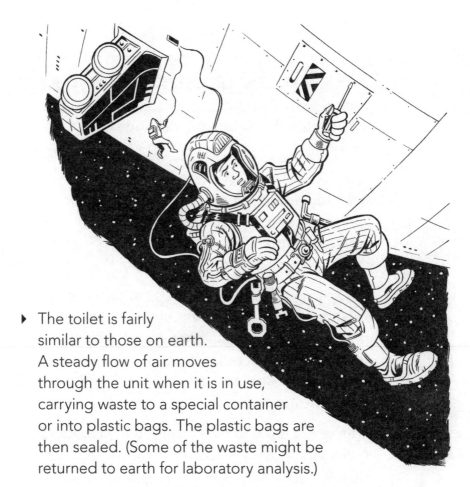

▸ The toilet is fairly
similar to those on earth.
A steady flow of air moves
through the unit when it is in use,
carrying waste to a special container
or into plastic bags. The plastic bags are
then sealed. (Some of the waste might be
returned to earth for laboratory analysis.)

▸ To wash, you will have a freshwater hose to
shower you and a vacuum hose to suck up all the
water. In other words you use vacuum cleaners
on yourself. You can't have a bath as the water
will float about. This is very dangerous as it might
short-circuit electrical equipment.

▸ As for brushing your teeth – that can be a challenge, too. You have to make sure the toothpaste is well down on the bristles and you have to stop the water from running away.

▸ You may have to perform spacewalks to complete your mission. This will involve getting into a spacesuit, which has been made to withstand flying debris and to protect astronauts from dramatic temperature changes (from –85°C in the shade to over 120°C in the hot sunlight).

▸ The spacesuit has a pressurized atmosphere, a source of oxygen, a means of removing carbon dioxide, a temperature regulator, some protection against radiation, and the means to communicate at all times with ground control or the space station.

▸ After going through depressurization procedures in the airlock, you'll step out into space. You are either attached by an air hose to the space station or you have a gas-propelled chair or unit that you can control so that you can go where you want, rather than drifting around helplessly.

Did You Know? The furthest distance that humans have ever travelled into space is 400,171 kilometres.

How To Rip A Phone Directory In Half

This is the ultimate test of strength – or is it just a matter of knowing how to do it? You decide:

1. With the spine of the book towards you, place your hands on top of the book and grip it with your little and ring fingers. Bend the book into a U shape by pushing with your thumbs.

2. Now hold the book tightly with all your fingers and, while keeping the U shape in place, bend the book the other way so that the pages form a V shape.

3. As you continue to bend the edges of the book down, the pages will start to split.

4. Push with one of your hands and pull with the other to rip the book in half.

HOW TO SERVE LIKE A WIMBLEDON CHAMPION

To perform the perfect tennis serve, remember three things: balance, timing and rhythm.

1. Grip the racket gently, spreading your fingers around the handle. Keep your arm relaxed. Take the ball in the other hand.

2. Face the net, point your racket at where you want the ball to go and use your throwing hand (this will be your left hand if you are right-handed) to support the ball.

3. Raise your hands together just a short way, then bring them down together. As you do this, start to turn your body so that you are sideways to the court. At the same time transfer your weight to your back foot.

4. Raise your throwing arm (left if you're right-handed) into an upright position to release the ball above your head. A good height to throw the ball is about 15 centimetres above your normal reach. Keep your arm straight and make sure you don't release the ball too soon or it will fly at an angle towards the net.

5. While the ball is in the air you need to bring the racket fluidly back and up, ready to hit the ball. At the same time as co-ordinating your arms you also need to transfer your weight from your back foot on to your front.

6. As the ball gets to the top of the throw, direct the racket at the ball in a swift throwing action. Aim to hit the ball with your racket arm straight, at the highest point you can reach it. The higher you make contact the more power you can generate and the harder and faster your serve.

7. Follow the motion through with your body, then look to recover quickly ready for your next shot.

How To Juggle

Take one ball and throw it from hand to hand. Make sure each throw goes straight up and to the same height (to just above eye level). Catch the ball at waist level.

Two Balls

Throw the first ball, **A**, as described above. Wait until it is about to descend and then throw the second ball, **B**, up underneath the first.

If you can't react quickly enough at first, try throwing the balls higher to give yourself more time to catch them.

If you find the balls are going forwards, throw them slightly in, towards yourself. Continue practising with the two balls until you feel confident. Then practise starting with your second hand.

Repeat these moves, throwing the balls higher as you grow more confident. Always have at least one ball in the air, and never more than one in either hand. Watch the balls as they reach their highest point and don't reach up to them, let them come down to you.

Three Balls

1. In your left hand hold ball **A** between your thumb, first and middle fingers, and ball **C** between your ring, little finger and your thumb. Ball **B** is in your right hand.

2. Throw ball **A** up; when it reaches its highest point, throw ball **B**. Catch ball **A** in your right hand.

3. When ball **B** reaches its highest point, throw ball **C**. Catch ball **B** in your left hand.

4. When ball **C** is at its highest point, throw ball **A**. Catch ball **C**. Throw ball **B** up and so on.

HOW TO REPAIR
A BICYCLE PUNCTURE

A bicycle is one of the best ways to get around – but would you know what to do if you were struck by a pesky puncture? Read on to discover how to fix one.

1. You'll need a puncture-repair kit, the bike manual and any necessary tools. Check the tyre for obvious causes of the flat – for example a nail or piece of glass.

2. Unscrew the valve to let any remaining air out of the tube. Remove the tyre from the wheel carefully so as not to pinch the tube.

3. Pull the tube out, pressing the valve through the hole in the rim (if it is secured with a rim nut, unscrew that first).

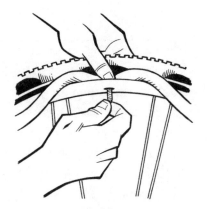

4. Look for the puncture. If it is not obvious, replace the valve, pump the tube up a little and listen for the hiss of escaping air, or dunk it in water. A stream of bubbles will reveal the site of the puncture.

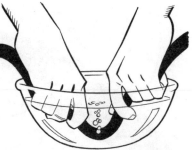

5. Once you've found the puncture, mark where it is with chalk. Making sure that the tube is completely dry, then lightly roughen the area round the puncture with fine sandpaper. This will allow the glue to bond better – don't be tempted to skip this step.

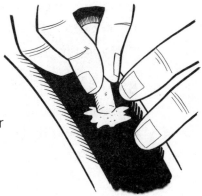

6. Apply a thin coat of rubber solution over the area where the leak is, covering an area slightly larger than the patch.

Allow it to dry completely – three to five minutes (be patient) – if you don't, the patch will probably come off.

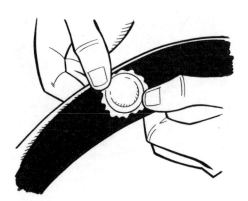

7. Take a patch of the right size and put a tiny blob of solution on its contact surface, then at once wipe it off with your finger, leaving a very thin coat.

Wait another three to five minutes. Then apply the patch, with the centre over the puncture, in one go (don't try to pull it off and reposition it), smoothing it down to get rid of any air bubbles. Press firmly.

8. Keep pressing it down really hard for at least a minute, especially round the edges. Wait for a couple of minutes and then carefully peel the backing paper or plastic off the patch.

If an edge of the patch lifts with it, quickly press it back down; then try lifting the backing again from the other side. If the whole patch comes away with the backing, you'll have to start again with a new patch. (Self-adhesive patches do exist – but they do not always work very well.)

9. Once you've removed the backing, press down on the patch to seal the edges – then it's time to replace the inner tube. Dust it with French chalk (from your puncture repair kit – grate it on your sandpaper), especially all round the patch so it doesn't stick to the inside of the tyre. That done, replace the valve and pump a little air into the tube; this makes it easier to replace.

10. As you replace the tube, make sure the valve stem is correctly positioned and that the tube is not pinched or creased. If everything looks okay then pump the tyre up to normal pressure. You've done it – but keep an eye on the tyre for a while.

If you keep getting punctures, check your tyres for wear. If they are very worn down, you are more likely to get a puncture, so replace your tyres regularly.

How To Win At Conkers

Conkers is a two-player game. Each player has a conker on a piece of string. The aim is to annihilate your opponent's conker before they destroy yours.

1. To prepare your conker, drill a hole through the centre from top to bottom. Then thread a piece of string 30 centimetres long through the hole. Tie a couple of knots below the conker to keep it in place.

2. Challenge a fellow conker-owner to a match and flip a coin to decide who will go first.

3. If your opponent goes first, wrap the end of your string tightly around your hand and let the conker dangle down.

Your opponent may then choose the height at which you hold the conker, and must try to hit it with his own. If he misses, he has two more attempts before it is your turn.

4. When it's your turn, keep the end of the string wrapped around your hand as before, then take the conker in your other hand and draw it back, ready to strike. Release the conker and swing it down as hard and fast as you can against your opponent's conker. Don't hurt yourself.

5. Continue taking it in turns to hit each other's conker until one of them is destroyed.

Tips For Winning

▸ Choose a big, symmetrical conker.

▸ Avoid conkers with cracks or white spots on them.

▸ Check that your conker sinks straight to the bottom of a glass of water, and discard any that float.

▸ Bake your conker in an oven.

▸ Soak your conker in vinegar.

▸ Coat your conker with a layer of matt varnish.

▸ Use a conker from a previous year.

HOW TO READ A COMPASS

Imagine the scene: you've been walking all day, and night is falling, but you've lost your bearings, and don't know which way to go to get home. This is when being able to read a compass comes in very handy (so long as you've got one with you). Here's how you do it.

1. Hold the compass flat in front of you so that the compass needle can float freely. The needle will point to magnetic north. (Do make sure there's nothing magnetic about, though – if, for instance, you had a magnet in your pocket the needle would point to that instead of to the north. Large metal objects – an iron gate, for instance – can also affect magnetic compasses.)

2. Rotate the compass housing until the orienting mark – N (for north) or the 0° symbol – lines up with the north end of the needle (which will be distinguished in some way, for example by being red).

3. Now you know where the magnetic north lies, which means that you now also know where south, east, west and all the other compass points are.

4. To use the compass to find your way to, say, a distant hill, aim the base plate of the compass so that the direction-of-travel line points exactly at the hill.

5. Turn the compass housing until the orienting mark is beneath the north end of the compass needle, then double-check to make sure that the direction-of-travel line is still pointing at the hill. You now have your bearings – and if you have taken them accurately, by following the direction-of-travel line while keeping the compass needle over the orienting mark, you will reach the hill.

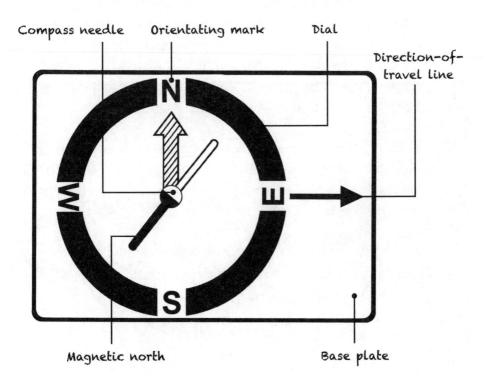

Compass needle   Orientating mark   Dial

Direction-of-travel line

Magnetic north   Base plate

How To Shake Off A Tail

The slang word for a person secretly following someone else to observe their movements is 'a tail'. Most amateur tails will follow behind you, trying not to be spotted. Here's how to lose one.

1. If you think you are being followed, occasionally stop as you walk around – perhaps to tie a shoelace, look for something in a pocket, and so on. Casually scan people behind you – and on the other side of the road – and make a rough note of anyone within distance, especially things such as height, colour of clothes, type of coat etc.;

look too for anyone you recognize from earlier on in your day. Stop again after a few hundred yards and take a casual glance round, as before – is anyone still there?

2. If there is, continue walking, but this time try going somewhere that most people would not go – use your ingenuity. Stop and look in shop windows, or pause to admire a shiny car (choose dark-coloured ones) – you can use the reflection on these surfaces to see who's behind you. Is there anyone whose reflection you recognize? If you're still not sure, try dawdling and then suddenly stop dead (as though you've suddenly forgotten something important) and let everyone else walk past – is there anyone who has also stopped and seems to be waiting?

3. Once you are certain you are being followed, make a note of what the person looks like. At the same time, make a plan for losing him or her.

4. When you are out of sight, change your own distinguishing features: if you're wearing a coat, take it off; if you're carrying a bag, hide it in your shirt; if you've got a hat in a pocket, put it on.

5. Speed up: do this not by quickening your pace, but by lengthening your strides – you'll travel a little bit further with every step.

6. Dodge about: enter a large shop and immediately leave by another exit; go down a narrow alley and, while out of sight of your tail, sprint round a corner and double back on your tracks, resuming your normal pace once you're back on a main street. Jump on a bus just as it's about to shut its doors – the possibilities are endless.

7. As a last resort, hide: dodge about until you're out of your tail's sight. The moment you are, duck into a deep doorway, crouch down behind a car, duck into the hallway of a large building – anywhere that he or she will hurry past, hoping to catch up with you. Remember, your tail will be anxious not to lose you, and in that state of mind will probably overlook something right under his or her nose.

How To Bend It Like Beckham

1. Approach the ball at an angle. Place your standing foot (rather than your kicking foot) close to the ball, facing the direction you want the ball to go. Start by practising this as you go to kick the ball.

2. Once you're comfortable with this, try to 'bend it'. If you kick with your right foot, to send the ball from right to left, strike the bottom half of the right-hand side with the inside, top half of your foot. To curve the ball from left to right, strike the bottom half of the left side of the ball with the outside of your foot. (Reverse these moves if you kick with your left foot.) To swerve a ball with the outside of your foot, strike 'across' the ball.

HOW TO KEEP PEOPLE IN SUSPENSE

A 'cliffhanger' is anything in a story, article, radio or TV programme, or film that leaves a listener, reader or viewer in suspense – the hero is left hanging from a cliff, in deadly danger of his life. It is a trick used to keep people's attention – by being kept in suspense, they want to know more.

You can use similar tricks to become the best teller (or writer) of jokes, stories, and even speeches, and hold your audience in suspense:

1. Don't give too much away too early. Quickly ending an account with something like 'Suddenly shots rang out and they all fell dead. The End' leaves people disappointed and frustrated.

2. Never rush. Spin the tale out (but don't go so slowly that it becomes boring). Pause occasionally – this often makes people say 'Go on!' or 'What happened next?'

3. Change direction. Just as you get to a good bit, say something like, 'Meanwhile, as the phantom bus bore down on us, Gran was making Eccles cakes at home …'

Leave people dangling just like this guy.

4. Break off your story occasionally. 'Then suddenly a huge black shape appeared in front of him and he – oh, there goes the bell. Tell you later.'

5. Leave the best part to the end, but build the drama up bit by bit.

Make sure the ending's worth waiting for – you won't be popular if you've kept people holding on, only for the finale to be a damp squib.

HOW TO JUMPSHOOT A BASKETBALL

You don't have to be as tall as Michael Jordan (a famous American basketball player) to jumpshoot a basketball. Just follow these handy hints and you'll be slamming that ball through the hoop in no time.

1. Start with both feet flat on the floor. With your body facing the basket, crouch down low – this will give you the momentum to jump.

2. Rise up off your feet. Make sure you can see the rim of the hoop. Your shooting hand should cup the ball and point towards the basket, while your other hand can gently guide the shot, loosely holding the side of the ball.

3. Keep your elbows in and your eyes on a spot over the front of the rim. Bend the wrist of your shooting hand backwards, the ball resting on the pads of your fingers.

4. As you spring off the ground, extend your arms, raising the ball smoothly in one fluid motion.

5. At the top of the jump, snap your wrist forward and let go of the ball.

6. At the end of the shot, when the ball flies through the hoop, your fingers should be pointing down to the floor.

How To Recognize A Witch

According to the children's author Roald Dahl, witches dress and look just like normal women. Luckily there are ways to spot a witch:

- They wear gloves because they have claws that need hiding.
- They are bald and wear wigs.
- They have larger nostrils than ordinary people.
- The pupil in the middle of their eyes changes colour from fire to ice.
- They don't have toes, so they have to wear wide shoes with square ends.
- They have blue spit.

HOW TO TELL WHICH WAY IS NORTH

You will need a wristwatch with hands, set to the correct local time. You need to be able to see the sun (even if it's shining through cloud). Most important of all, you also need to know that the sun rises in the east and sets in the west; and that at 12 noon in the northern hemisphere it is due south (in the southern hemisphere it's due north).

1. With the watch horizontal, aim the hour hand at the sun. An angle is created between the hour hand and the 12 on the watch face. Divide this angle in two. The line that follows the angle that you've created is the north-south line (see the picture on page 201). Since you know the position of the sun at noon, and you know the time, you can then work out which way is north and which is south.

2. If you have a digital watch, draw a watch face on a piece of paper, mark the 12 and then draw in the hour hand in the position for the time shown on your digital. Next, aim the hour hand in the drawing at the sun and follow the procedure as for a watch with hands (technically termed an analogue watch).

3. If you are in the southern hemisphere, aim the 12 on the watch face at the sun and find the north-south line by bisecting the angle between the hour hand and 12. Remember that in this hemisphere, the sun will be due north at noon; otherwise, exactly the same principles apply as for the northern hemisphere.

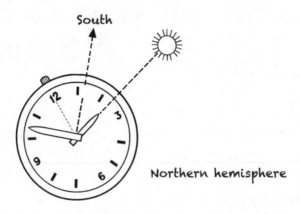

HOW TO WARM YOUR FEET

Sprinkle a pinch of ground cayenne pepper into your socks. It will warm your feet without burning them. But be sure that any cuts, blisters and scratches on your feet are covered with a sticking plaster, and be very careful not to allow the pepper to touch your eyes, or the nose and mouth area, as it might sting or at least feel uncomfortably hot.

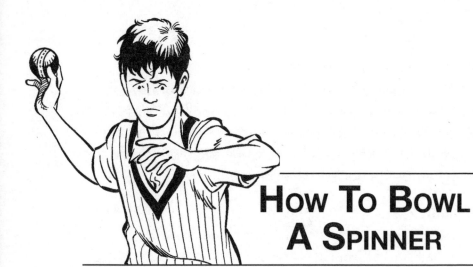
HOW TO BOWL A SPINNER

Spin bowling is one of the most skilful bowling techniques in the game of cricket. The spin bowler uses the wrist and fingers to make the ball spin as it leaves the hand. The spin causes the ball to change direction once it lands. This makes it harder for the batsman to hit the ball, and can sometimes turn the ball from its path on to the wicket. In addition, a spinning ball may often come off the bat at an unpredictable angle, leading to the batsman being caught out.

There are two main types of spin bowling – off-spin and leg-spin.

General Tips

Play with a cricket ball as often as you can – throw it up and down, twisting your wrist to make the ball spin in the air. Bear in mind that you can probably get more spin with a worn ball, so when playing a match try not to use a brand-new ball. When bowling, keep your arms close to your body. Bring your bowling arm down quickly and release the ball as high as you can, so the flight of the ball causes the batsman to lift his head up and then down, which may put him off his stroke.

Off-Spin

Twist your hand in a clockwise direction as you let go of the ball so that when it hits the pitch it spins to your right. The spin is generated by the three middle fingers, with the middle joints of your fingers resting on the seam of the ball. As you bowl, turn your wrist clockwise to generate the spin on the ball. Use your first two fingers to deliver the ball.

Leg-Spin

Twist the ball anti-clockwise and release it from the palm so that it rolls over the base of your little finger. It will spin to your left when it lands. Hold the ball with the top joints of the index and second fingers across the seam, the ball resting between a bent third finger and the thumb. As you release the ball, straighten your fingers; much of the work on the ball will be done by the third finger, turning the ball anti-clockwise. Flick your wrist so your palm faces downwards.

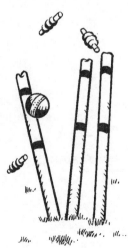

HOW TO CUSTOMIZE YOUR T-SHIRT

However cool your T-shirt is, chances are that someone will have the same one. A great way to make sure you really stand out (and have lots of fun, too) is to create your very own designer shirt.

You Will Need:
- a plain T-shirt
- 2 pieces thick cardboard
- a pencil
- a marker pen
- scissors
- fabric paint
- a paintbrush
- old newspaper
- sticky tape.

To make this cool 'crazy face' T-shirt you are going to make a stencil using one of your pieces of cardboard. A stencil is a cut-out shape used to paint your image on to your T-shirt, so when you're finished, the face will be printed on to your T-shirt in one, bright, bold colour.

What You Do

1. Take one of your pieces of cardboard and make sure that it is big enough to cover the T-shirt. Using the pencil, draw the shape of the eyes and the mouth on to the card.

2. Fill in the shapes you have drawn using the marker pen, this will give you an idea of what your finished T-shirt will look like.

3. Carefully cut the shape out of the cardboard. Poke the scissors through the centre of the tongue and start from this hole, working outwards to the outline of the mouth and tongue until you have a mouth-shaped hole in the cardboard.

Do the same for the eyes, first cutting around the outer black line, and then the inner line. You will be left with two smaller pieces of cardboard that fit inside the eyes – do not throw these away. Ask an adult to help you if you find this tricky.

4. Place your T-shirt on some sheets of old newspaper and put the other piece of card inside the shirt. This card stops the paint going through to the back of the T-shirt.

5. Put your stencil on top of the T-shirt so the picture is where you want it to be and tape it in place. Make sure you tape the centres of the eyes in place too, using loops of sticky tape.

6. Now, carefully brush the fabric paint on to the T-shirt. By using the stencil, the paint only goes on to the part of the shirt where the cut-out shape is.

7. Leave the stencil taped to the shirt for a couple of hours while the paint dries and then carefully remove it. Your new 'crazy face' T-shirt is now ready to wear.

HOW TO SIGNAL A PLANE

If you've ever watched planes landing at an airport, you may have spotted someone in high-visibility clothing and ear protectors waving their arms at the pilot. These people are called ground controllers, and their job is to guide planes around the airport once they have safely landed.

Ground controllers communicate with pilots using a series of signals that are understood by aviators all around the world. Each signal has to be clearly executed so there is no danger of the pilot getting confused and steering his plane in the wrong direction.

Here are the ten most commonly used signals. So, next time you're at an airport, you'll know exactly what's going on.

Start engines   All clear

Normal stop

Emergency stop

Turn right

Turn left

Proceed straight ahead

Slow down

Fire (left arm indicates
the location of fire)

Cut engines

How To Boil An Egg

If you want to be sure you never starve, learn how to rustle up a delicious soft-boiled egg. You could even earn some extra pocket money by making your parents a boiled egg with toast for breakfast in bed.

Be Prepared

Take your eggs out of the fridge about 20 minutes before you boil them. If you take eggs straight from the fridge and put them into boiling water, they are quite likely to crack.

If you forget to take your eggs out of the fridge in time and you are in a hurry, run them under a warm tap for a minute.

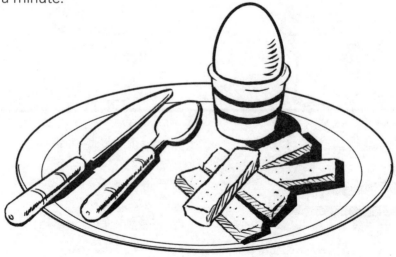

Don't choose really fresh eggs to boil – you will find that their shells are hard to peel off once they are boiled. Instead choose eggs that are roughly five days old.

Find a saucepan just large enough for the eggs you want to boil. If you use a pan that is too large, your eggs may move around and crack against each other or on the side of the pan.

What You Do

1. Pour some cold water in the saucepan. Bring the water to the boil.

2. Put a small pinprick in each of the eggs. This allows any steam to exit and will prevent cracking.

3. Place each egg on a spoon and gently lower into the saucepan.

4. Reduce the heat so the water is no longer boiling but 'simmering' (bubbling gently).

5. Set your timer. The length of time you cook each egg depends on how you (or your folks) like their eggs.

Timing

If you are using large or medium-sized eggs, cook your eggs for exactly three minutes – this will give you a perfectly-cooked egg with a deliciously runny yolk. If you are boiling extra-large eggs, five minutes' cooking will leave the yolk runny. Seven minutes will mean it is only very slightly runny.

6. Once the cooking time is up, carefully pick up each egg with the spoon and pop them in eggcups, with the rounder end of the egg at the bottom. Serve with buttered toast soldiers (pieces of toast cut up into strips), perfect for dipping into that delectably runny yolk. Don't forget the salt and pepper.

How To Save The World

You don't have to be a science supremo or a mathematics maestro to be able to save the world. Instead, you can do lots of small, simple things to help look after the environment and protect the planet. Not convinced? Read on …

1. Walk or cycle to school instead of being driven.

2. Save electricity by switching off appliances when you are not using them – don't just leave them on standby.

3. Recycle everything you can – either by reusing items for other purposes or by taking them to recycling banks.

4. Take an interest in environmental issues: on television, in newspapers and on the Internet.

5. Take out reusable bags when shopping, and refuse new ones when offered.

6. Take quick showers instead of deep baths.

7. Use energy-efficient light bulbs.

How To Maximize Your Pocket Money

However much pocket money your parents give you, one thing is almost certain – it's never enough for all the wonderful things you want to buy. Read on to find out how you can boost the money in your pocket.

The best way to do this is to find something that people will pay you to do. For example, most adults have cars, and it's fairly certain that a lot of these cars will need cleaning. This creates an opportunity for you to earn some money.

If you do a really good job, people will ask you to clean their cars again. They may even tell other people how good you are.

Planning

▸ Identify your customers. Parents, relatives and neighbours may all need their cars cleaned. Make sure you ask your parents' permission before you start and always tell them if you are going out to clean someone's car.

▸ Decide on your price. The best way to get customers is to offer a lower price than your rivals. If your local garage has a car wash, check how much it costs and offer a lower price to your customers.

Washing The Car

You Will Need:
- 2 buckets
- some car shampoo
- a sponge
- a stiff brush
- a 'chamois' leather (pronounced 'shammy')
- a lot of water
- a hose, if you have one.

> **Warning.** You will get wet while washing cars, so wear some old clothes or overalls to cover your clothes.

What You Do

There are six steps to a thorough clean:

1. Fill one bucket with warm water mixed with car shampoo and the other bucket with clean water.

2. Rinse the car with the clean water to remove surface dirt.

3. Dip your brush into the warm, soapy water and give the wheels a good scrub.

4. Clean the rest of the car by dipping the sponge into the soapy water and rubbing the car by moving the sponge in a circular motion. Start at the roof and work downwards.

5. When you have finished, rinse the car with clean water again.

6. Dry the car with the chamois leather.

> If you use a hose for rinsing, it will make the job quicker and easier. Make sure all the car doors are shut before you turn the hose on though – you don't want to give the inside of the car a drenching.

How To Undo A Jammed Jar Lid

Impress your family and friends with your strength and skill at undoing the most stubborn of jam-jar lids.

Hot Water

If the lid is made of metal, run hot water over it for about 20 seconds (take care not to scald yourself). Alternatively, fill a basin with hot water and stand the jar in it upside down, so the water covers the lid completely. Never use boiling water as it might cause the glass of the jar to crack.

Dry the lid thoroughly with a towel. Pop on some rubber washing-up gloves (to help you grip) and twist the lid.

Open Sesame

If the lid is still stuck, turn the jar upside down and carefully bang the lid firmly on a hard surface. Repeat this two or three times, then turn the jar the right way up and twist the lid. It should easily come undone.

HOW TO BE A RODEO STAR

Howdy, Partner! So, you want to ride the rodeo? Well, if you're very brave and a little bit crazy, then saddle up, cowboy. You've got some broncos to ride.

The sport known today as 'rodeo' began in the 1800s, when cowboys working on ranches in America's Wild West would display their skills in rounding up herds of cattle for branding. Nowadays, rodeo is considered a highly competitive sport, with cowboys and cowgirls fighting to stay on their bucking and rearing horses to have a chance of winning big prize money.

Ride 'Em Cowboy!
First, get yourself a horse or a bull. If you don't fancy the idea of riding a bull, stick to horses for now. It has to be a horse that isn't accustomed to being ridden. The horse is kept in a pen beside the rodeo ring (called the 'chute') to keep it still until you are ready to ride. While it is in the chute, check to make sure the saddle, stirrups and reins are fixed securely – you're going to need them.

Put your left foot in the left stirrup, grab the saddle with your left hand, and pull yourself up on to the horse, swinging your right leg over and into the right stirrup.

Now, as if rodeo riding wasn't difficult enough, the rules only allow you to hold the reins with one hand.

The gate of the chute will open and you're off. As soon as you get on the horse, it will arch its back, leap into the air and try to throw you off.

All you have to do is to hold on. If you can stay on the horse for eight seconds, you've completed the ride. Try to ride with style, as you score points for how well you ride, and the person with the most points at the end is the winner. Holding one arm (the one that isn't busy hanging on to the reins) high in the air looks really cool.

Be careful not to touch the horse with your free hand, as this will get you disqualified from the competition.

Try and find a rhythm as the horse bucks and rears, and move your body with this rhythm to stay balanced. Shout, 'Yee-ha!' and 'Ride 'em, cowboy!' as often as possible – you don't get any points for this, but it's fun.

Finally, if you've managed to stay on the bronco, a 'pick up rider' will ride up next to you and help you get off.

If you are skilful enough to have scored the most points during your bucking bronco ride, then congratulations! You will be awarded some prize money and you'll get a much sought-after engraved, silver rodeo belt buckle.

Rodeo Repartee

It's also important to talk like a rodeo star. Here are a few terms to get you started:

▸ **Biting The Dust.** Being thrown off the horse.

▸ **Bronco.** A horse that isn't 'broken' – that isn't trained to have a rider on its back.

▸ **High Roller.** A horse that jumps high when it tries to buck you off.

▸ **Tenderfoot.** Someone who is new to the rodeo.

How To Breakdance

isten up. It's time to step up and pull some seriously slammin' shapes. Here's a move that requires plenty of practice and, more importantly, bags of confidence. Once you've mastered the steps below you can begin to improvise, creating your own personal breakdancing style.

1. Place your hands on the floor a little more than shoulder-width apart. Your legs should be spread a little wider.

2. Lift your right hand up and bring your left leg forward to the place where your right hand was.

3. Now bend your right leg behind your left leg, so that your right foot is almost directly under your bottom.

4. Next, you need to uncross your legs, keeping your right leg where it is and swinging your left leg out and under your bottom.

5. Shift your weight on to your right arm (the more of your weight that is on your hand, the faster your feet can move). Keeping your left leg where it is, swing your right leg in front and across your left leg, as shown.

6. Keeping your right hand where it is, step back with your left leg. This is the bit that will need some practice to perfect.

7. Now, simply put your right leg back into the starting position and put your left hand on the floor. Now repeat the six steps.

Now show your crew what you can do!

Don't try and do this move quickly until you can do the steps without having to think too hard. You should soon be able to make it look smooth and effortless.

How To Brew Your Own Ginger Beer

When you've been running around in the sunshine, there's no better refreshment than an ice-cold glass of good old-fashioned ginger beer, and it's even better when you've made it yourself. This recipe will make enough ginger beer to fill a large bottle.

You Will Need:
- 450ml water
- 2 heaped tablespoons fresh ginger, peeled and finely chopped
- a lemon
- 250g sugar
- ½ teaspoon cream of tartar
- 800ml cold water
- ½ teaspoon dried yeast
- a saucepan
- a knife
- a cloth (to cover the saucepan)
- string or a large elastic band
- a large, clean plastic bottle
- a sieve
- a measuring jug.

What You Do
1. Measure 450 millilitres of water into a saucepan.

2. Cut the lemon into thick slices and add the slices to the pan with the chopped ginger.

3. Add the sugar and the cream of tartar.

4. Bring your mixture to the boil, stirring it slowly. Then turn the heat down and let it simmer (boil gently) for five minutes.

Warning. Ask an adult to help you when you are heating the mixture.

5. Add the 800 millilitres of cold water and immediately remove the pan from the heat, then sprinkle the yeast over your mixture.

6. Let the pan cool for five minutes, then put a cloth over the top of it and tie it round with string or a large elastic band so it does not touch the water. The mixture now needs to be left for 24 hours. It doesn't need to go in the fridge, but keep it out of direct sunlight.

7. You need a clean plastic bottle for your ginger beer. A 1½ litre plastic cola bottle is fine, but it is very important to clean it thoroughly with hot water. Make sure you use a plastic bottle as glass ones can explode.

8. Strain your mixture through a sieve into a measuring jug and then pour it into the plastic bottle. It is also very important that you leave some empty space at the top of the bottle for the build-up of fizzy gas.

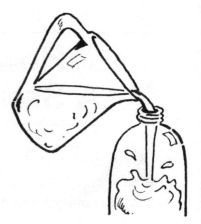

9. Put the lid on your bottle and leave it for two days. About four times each day, unscrew the lid a little bit to let the gas out and then screw it on again.

10. Your ginger beer should now be ready to drink. Chill it in the fridge for a while so it's nice and cold before you drink it. Make sure you drink it within three days, while it's still fresh.

How To Write
A Secret Message

All top secrets are best kept and passed in code. Devising your own code to use with a friend is the best way of ensuring no one will crack it:

1. Break your message into groups of two letters:

I am the best at everything

ia mt he be st at ev er yt hi ng

2. Then reverse the letters in each pair:

ai tm eh eb ts ta ve re ty ih gn

3. Now run the letters together:

aitmehebtstaveretyihgn

Think about how you could adapt this code: adding a dummy letter between each pair of letters, swapping adjacent pairs, or reversing every other pair.

How To Ride Bareback

Ever imagined yourself riding bareback into the sunset like cowboys do in the movies? Before Hollywood comes knocking at your door you'll need to learn how.

Professional Instruction

It is essential to learn to ride bareback with an experienced rider or trained instructor, and to wear all the appropriate safety gear. However, here are some tips to remember.

▸ Choose a horse with a smooth riding action, a broad back and low 'withers' (the ridges between a horse's shoulder blades). All these factors make it easier for you to stay on the horse.

▸ Before attempting to ride bareback, practise riding with a saddle but without stirrups – this is a great way to prepare.

▸ Wear some extra padding in your trousers – bareback riding can be painful!

Riding Bareback

1. Use a fixed platform to mount your horse. Once you're astride, take your time to get settled and balanced.

2. When you are ready, take the reins. Set off, making sure your instructor is walking beside you, leading the horse.

3. When you're under way, keep your head up and eyes focused on where you are heading. Don't look down, as this might make you sway on the horse's back.

4. Keep your legs long and relaxed, as if your body is sinking down through the horse's back. Resist the temptation to clench your thighs too much. Avoid digging your heels into the sides of your horse.

5. Keep your back straight. Try not to lean back, as this will push your legs too far forwards. If you lean forwards, your heels will also be in the wrong position.

6. If you feel you are slipping, don't grip your horse with your legs, this will only cause it to move faster. Ride 'em, cowboy!

HOW TO BE TOP DOG

Although you can actually teach an old dog new tricks, there's no doubt that it's easier to train and improve the obedience of a puppy. If you are lucky enough to get a puppy this is a great opportunity for you to spend some quality time with the fluffiest member of your family. What's more, by putting in some effort at the start, your puppy will be sure to grow up knowing that you are top dog.

Lie Down

1. Get your puppy to sit in front of you while you hold its collar. Have a treat in your hand and show it to the puppy.

2. Lower the treat towards the ground so that your puppy must move its whole body downwards to keep its eyes on the treat. Keep hold of your puppy's collar so it can't gobble it up.

3. Say 'down' clearly, as your puppy begins to move downwards.

4. If you're having trouble, you can encourage your puppy by gently picking up its front legs and lowering it to the ground. Don't forget to restate the command 'down' while you are doing this.

5. Once your puppy is lying on the floor, give it the treat.

6. Keep repeating the exercise but replace the reward with ear-tickling, neck-scratching and generally making a big fuss every time your puppy obeys.

Good Dog!

▸ **Short And Fun.** Keep your training sessions short and fun so your furry friend enjoys each lesson.

▸ **Keep It Simple.** Give your puppy one, clear instruction to follow – it is just a young animal and will not be able to cope with anything unclear. Repeat every task again and again to make sure it sticks in your puppy's memory.

▸ **Be Consistent.** Your puppy will be confused if you change your mind. So, if he or she is not allowed upstairs on your bed, make it clear that they must not go on the beds – ever!

▸ **Good Dog.** Be positive and offer lots of encouragement (and rewards) to your puppy. Don't punish bad behaviour but make it clear that it won't be tolerated. Always reward good behaviour with plenty of cuddles.

How To Annoy People In A Lift

You know you're a funny guy, right? Well, even top comedians need to practise their hilarious gags. A lift is the perfect place to brush up on your humour, as your audience can't go anywhere. Try out these tips and see how long their patience holds out.

▸ Salute and say, 'Welcome aboard!' every time someone gets into the lift.

▸ Sit down and start barking like a dog.

▸ Ask everyone for a high-five at each floor.

- Pretend to be a flight attendant. Tell people how to fasten their seatbelts, where the nearest exits are, and what happens if the lift lands on water.

- Suggest a game of charades, and act things out.

- Open your bag and, while looking inside, say, 'I'll get you some food as soon as I can.'

- Spin around and around in the centre of the lift.

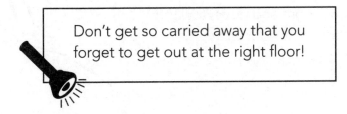

Don't get so carried away that you forget to get out at the right floor!

HOW TO BE A YO-YO STAR

If you have mastered the basic up and down yo-yo motion, it's time to turn on the star quality as you master a 'Sleeper' and 'Walk The Dog'.

You will need a good quality yo-yo and some serious practice to master the moves described below.

The Sleeper

The idea of the Sleeper is to gain enough control of your yo-yo so that, instead of bouncing back up to you, the yo-yo 'sleeps'.

1. Hold the yo-yo in your palm with the back of your hand facing downwards.

2. Bend your arm up towards your shoulder and, as you straighten it, smoothly release the yo-yo from your hand, flicking it out and down towards the floor with your wrist.

3. When the yo-yo reaches its lowest point, keep your hand still for a while. This will ensure the yo-yo 'sleeps' at the end of the string, still spinning but not coming back up.

4. After a few seconds, turn your hand palm down and jerk the yo-yo back up.

Walk The Dog

1. Throw a Sleeper towards a flat floor. When the yo-yo is 'sleeping', lower it on to the floor.

2. As soon as the yo-yo makes contact with the floor it will start rolling away from you. Tug the string to bring the yo-yo up to your hand.

How To Win
A Nobel Prize

Having decided to become the best, the top award to aim for is a Nobel Prize, awarded since 1901 for great achievements in Physics, Chemistry, Medicine, Literature, Economics and Peace.

A Swedish scientist, named Alfred Nobel, gave some of his fortune to be used as prizes for the awards. He had become rich by inventing dynamite. He spent years experimenting and managed to blow up quite a few people – including his younger brother – along the way! Here is your very own step-by-step guide to winning one of these prestigious awards.

Eyes On The Prize

1. Work hard at school. Don't worry, this is the boring bit – it gets better from now on.

2. Make sure you become a scientist, writer, economist or worker for peace (there's no Nobel Prize for football, unfortunately).

3. Now for the tricky bit. You need to do something special:

▸ For the science awards, your best bet is to invent
  or discover something. This should be something
  useful. A cure for a disease is really good;
  inventing a clockwork toenail clipper is much less
  likely to get you noticed. Whatever you invent, try
  very hard not to blow up any younger brothers
  during your experiments.

▸ For the Literature Prize, you need to write some
  wonderful books. Keep reading regularly to see
  what your favourite authors are writing about,
  and get some inspiration from them.

▸ The Economics Prize is yours if you can come up
  with new theories about how the world of money
  works, or should work.

▸ The best way to win the Nobel Peace Prize is
  to find a war and stop it. This is quite a tricky
  thing to do, but probably won't involve as much
  homework as the other Nobel Prizes you might
  be aiming for.

What Next?

▸ You have to wait for someone to nominate you. This has to be someone such as a famous scientist or a university professor. Unfortunately you can't just get your best friend to do it.

▸ Sit by the phone. The call comes just before the awards are announced to the world.

▸ Pack your passport and some warm clothing (the ceremony is in December) and catch a plane to Stockholm in Sweden.

▸ Collect your award. Each Nobel Prize winner receives a Nobel Prize diploma, a Nobel Prize medal (made of real gold), and prize money.

▸ Bask in your glory and feel very pleased with yourself.

Of course, if you really want to show off, there's no need to stop at one Nobel Prize. Marie Curie, a Polish scientist, won two, her husband won one, her daughter, Irene, won one, and her other daughter's husband won one, too.

HOW TO MAKE A STINK

Other than the obvious way, that is … You can buy stink bombs, but here's how to make your own.

You Will Need:
- an egg
- a drop of milk
- ½ teaspoon sugar
- a tin or plastic food container with a lid that can be shut tight.

Note. If using a plastic container, choose one made of bendy rather than rigid plastic, which could crack.

1. Break the egg into the container, add the milk and sugar and shut your container tight. Put it in a warm, sunny place, preferably outdoors. If it has to be indoors, hide it near a boiler or radiator. Leave it for two weeks.

2. After two weeks use a suitable instrument to make about 20 holes in the lid of the container.

3. Now find a good place to hide your creation. Soon a delightful stink will waft out, and you can enjoy watching everyone looking for the source of the revolting smell.

It is best to avoid letting stink bombs off at school. Your teachers will not be impressed!

HOW TO MAKE
A MISSISSIPPI MUD PIE

The Mississippi mud pie is a seriously chocolatey cake. Its name comes from its likeness to the muddy banks of the Mississippi river where the cake was invented. To make your own deliciously messy pie follow the simple recipe below.

You Will Need:
For The Crumb Base:
- 100g crushed digestive biscuits
- 50g butter, melted
- 25g demerara sugar

For The Filling:
- 400g dark chocolate
- 225g butter
- 2 tablespoons boiling water
- 350g dark muscovado sugar
- 300ml single cream
- 6 eggs
- a 20cm diameter loose-bottomed cake tin
- … oh, and a squirt of whipped cream.

What You Do

1. Preheat the oven to 190°C (Gas Mark 5). Grease your cake tin with a bit of butter.

> **Warning.** Always get an adult to supervise when using an oven.

2. To make the base, mix together the melted butter, crushed biscuits and demerara sugar. Spoon the mix into the bottom of your cake tin and flatten it down.

3. To make the filling, take a small saucepan filled with water to a depth of five centimetres, and place it on the hob and bring to the boil. Place a heatproof mixing bowl inside the saucepan. Break the chocolate into the bowl and stir in the butter and the two tablespoons of boiling water. Stir until completely melted.

4. Remove the bowl from the heat and beat in the single cream and muscovado sugar. Whisk in the eggs quickly to avoid scrambling them!

5. Pour the mixture into the tin, on top of the crumb base. Bake for an hour and 15 minutes or until the top is crunchy.

6. Allow to cool before carefully removing the cake from the tin. Serve with a squirt of whipped cream. Mmmm …

HOW TO BE A SOUND-EFFECTS WIZARD

A sound-effects engineer can play tricks with your ears by creating a convincing sound to accompany an action. If they have done their job well, you will not suspect any deception has taken place.

It's a great job – but have you got what it takes to become a sound-effects wizard? A real sound-effects engineer will have a range of complex electronic equipment at his fingertips and a studio to work from, but you don't need either of these. The key to producing great sound effects is being creative and using whatever is around you to create the noise that you need.

Here are some convincing sound effects you can generate using simple everyday objects. Try some of the following stunts on your friends and family and see if they fall for your sound effects.

▸ Complain to your mum that your finger is hurting so much that you are determined to saw it off. Disappear from view (but stay within earshot), and saw a raw cabbage in half with a serrated knife (one with a jagged edge). This will produce the desired hair-raising sound and your mum will soon come running. Make sure you're careful when using knives.

▸ You are out in the garden, when you and a friend spot a huge beetle walking along the ground. As you're friend looks away, pretend to step on the beetle (make sure you don't actually harm the beetle by mistake). As you step, scrunch a bag of potato crisps hidden behind your back. Your friend will believe you have actually trodden on the beetle if you have done it successfully.

▸ Your mum hands you an important letter to drop in the postbox on your way to school. As your mum turns away, bring the edge of the letter up to your lips and blow hard – so your breath rushes along the front and back of the letter. At the same time move your hands as if you are tearing something in two. If you get it right, the sound you make should be the same as if you had ripped the letter in half. Wait for the look on your mum's face.

‣ Complain to your dad that your kid brother or sister is annoying you. Move so you are standing directly between your dad's line of vision and your sibling, then turn and slap your own forearm sharply. Your dad will be convinced you have whacked your brother/sister.

‣ For an embarrassing sound, as your friend sits down in a chair, rub your hand across an inflated, wet balloon – the effect is very funny indeed!

HOW TO FIND THE LOCH NESS MONSTER

Loch Ness, home to the legendary Loch Ness Monster, or 'Nessie', is a deep, dark lake in northern Scotland. There have been many reported sightings and even a few photographs of the monster, although no one is sure whether the shapes photographed in the loch are actually of the famous beast or if they are clever fakes. Follow these top tips and maybe you'll be the first to find this mythical monster:

▸ Find a speedboat and get out on to the water. A boat fitted with sonar equipment is perfect. Sonar allows you to search deep in the water by sending out pulses of sound and recording any objects they bounce off. If Nessie is lurking under the water, sonar will help you find it.

▸ According to Nessie experts, the monster mainly eats fish, so take some with you to offer as presents if you see it, and show it that you mean no harm.

▸ Keep your camera with you at all times. If you do spot Nessie, no one will believe you unless you've got photographic evidence.

How To Beat The Clock When You Get Up

You never know when you might need to get dressed in a hurry. Next time you sleep through your alarm, these tips will save you valuable seconds.

▸ **Choose Your Clothes The Night Before.** Choose what you're going to wear when you're wide awake – and save time rooting around in your wardrobe in the morning while you're half-asleep.

▸ **Take Your Clothes Off Carefully.** If you have to wear a shirt and tie for school, loosen your tie but keep it knotted and hanging around your shirt collar. Undo the top two buttons of the shirt, keeping everything together. Tomorrow you can pop both over your head in a hurry.

▸ **Keep Layers Intact.** If you're wearing a T-shirt and jumper, always pull both off at the same time – not one by one. That way you will be able to pull them on again all in one go tomorrow morning.

▸ **Keep Some Clothes On.** If it's cold, just put on a clean pair of socks at night. That's one less thing to do tomorrow!

HOW TO TELL
A GOOD JOKE

Question: What is the king of the hankies called?
Answer: The 'hanki'-chief!

Okay, so that joke's not likely to bring the house down, but some people are able to tell any joke and get their audience to laugh. How? By following these dos and don'ts.

Things You Should Do

▸ **DO** know your joke back-to-front and inside out. How many times have people started to tell you a joke then stopped because they can't remember the story or the punchline?

▸ **DO** pace yourself. Never rush through your joke. Be confident. Your audience will share your enjoyment and be more likely to laugh at the end.

▸ **DO** keep your jokes short. It's hard to hold an audience's attention for more than two minutes.

▸ **DO** be confident. Keep your delivery lively.

▸ **DO** make the punchline strong. Try to stay confident right through to the end of the joke. Your audience is waiting patiently for the killer ending that will make them roar with laughter, so don't let them down by fluffing the punchline.

▸ **DO** build up a collection of good jokes. Copy any joke that makes you laugh from friends or professionals, and adapt them to suit you.

Things You Shouldn't Do

▸ **DON'T** try to tell jokes in strange accents unless you can do them really well. At best, your accent might confuse the audience. At worst, it might offend people.

▸ **DON'T** tell just any joke. Choose one that suits your audience and their interests.

▸ **DON'T** be put off if your audience doesn't like your jokes. Listen to which bits they do laugh at and next time leave out the bits that got groaned at or booed.

How To Raise Someone Up Using 'Finger Power'

How strong are your friends? Strong enough to lift you off the ground using only their fingers? No? Well, follow these instructions and you'll be amazed by your friends' incredible, superhuman strength.

What You Do

1. You need four friends to lift you with their 'power fingers'. Sit on a chair without arms, such as a school chair. Sit very still and stay relaxed.

2. Two of your friends should stand behind the chair, the third should stand at the right-hand side of the chair and the fourth at the left-hand side.

3. Ask one of your friends to place his left hand on top of your head. Your three other friends should then place their left hands on top of his. Ask your friends to do the same with their right hands so that all eight hands are resting on your head.

4. The lifters must now concentrate. While thinking about raising you into the air, they should chant the following aloud 20 times: 'Light as a feather! Stiff as a board!'

5. The lifters should now remove their hands and then each press their left and right hands together, with both their index fingers sticking out and the others clasped round each other, as shown here.

6. The two people at either side of the chair put these two fingers under each of your knees. The two people standing behind the chair place their fingers under your armpits.

7. Count to three out loud. When you call out 'three', everybody should lift upwards with their fingers. Incredibly, you will lift up as if you really were as light as a feather. Your friends will be able to lift you quite high, but make sure they let you down again carefully and gently.

> Quite often, it takes two or three goes to get this to work properly. If it does not work first time, remember to start again from the beginning and repeat the chanting.

How To Win A Bet

The next time you want to win a bet with your best mate, why not try this trick?

You Will Need:
- 500g cornflour
- water
- a large mixing bowl
- a pound coin
- a wristwatch or stopwatch.

What You Do

1. Pour the cornflour into the bowl. Slowly add some water and stir the mixture until you get a thick, custard-like consistency.

2. Invite your friend into the kitchen and show him the mixture.

3. Ask him to give you a pound coin and find one of your own. Drop both coins into the bowl.

4. Now challenge your friend to put his hand in and grab one coin within five seconds. If he manages it, he can keep both coins. If he doesn't, you will keep them.

5. Time five seconds and see how he gets on.

The Victory

You will find that the quicker your friend attempts to grab the money, the faster and harder the mixture will set around his hand. This should make it impossible to fish out either of the coins.

To show him how it is done, put your hand into the mix very s-l-o-w-l-y, find a coin and slowly take it out.

Practise your technique beforehand to get your time down to five seconds or less. Remember, the slower your hand moves around in the mixture, the easier it will be to fish out the coin.

How To Putt Like A Pro

You're out on the golf course, and victory in a tournament is within your grasp – and all you have to do is sink a putt. What do you do?

Don't Rush

Take time to 'read' the green (the smooth, grassy area around the hole). Look for dips, mounds and other contours. Try to visualize the route you want your ball to take from the moment you hit it until it goes into the hole.

The Right Position

Stand sideways-on to the hole. Your shoulders should be at right angles to the shaft of your club. Balance your weight equally on both feet to keep your body stable. You should be near enough to the ball to hit it without being cramped or leaning forwards. Always keep the blade at the bottom of your golf club flat.

The Right Putting Motion

Grip the club in the palms of your hands, not with your fingers. Hold it firmly, but don't squeeze, as this will cause your shoulders to tense up which will affect the smoothness of your swing. You need to keep this steady grip throughout the putting action to make sure you keep your stroke smooth.

As you take your putt, your shoulders should move back as you raise the club and then forwards as you swing your arm to hit the ball. You should not flip or twist your hands when you putt.

The Glove Trick

If you need extra power for a long or uphill putt, it's very easy to lose control of your arms and shoulders – which spells disaster for your putt. To stop this happening, tuck a glove under the armpit of the arm that is closest to the hole. You should be able to keep the glove in place throughout the stroke.

Aim For A Small Target

Practising your putting action is essential. Stick two tees in the ground about 10 centimetres apart (tees are the small plastic stands that keep the ball from rolling around before you take a shot). Now aim to putt the ball between them. This is harder than sinking a ball into a hole, because any putts that are slightly off centre will just bounce off the tees. When you're out on the course, you'll find the holes seem much wider and you will be more likely to sink a ball.

You will also love …

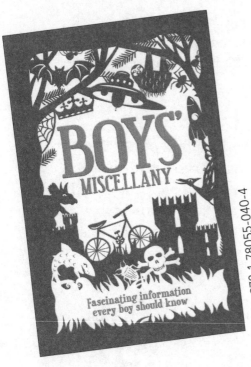

ISBN: 978-1-78055-040-4

ISBN: 978-1-78055-178-4